Alternative Dispute Resolution in the Construction Industry

An Evaluation of UK Research and Practice

By
Andrew Agapiou

Alternative Dispute Resolution in the Construction Industry: An Evaluation of UK Research and Practice
By Andrew Agapiou

This book first published 2023
Ethics International Press Ltd, UK
British Library Cataloguing in Publication Data
A catalogue record for this book is available from the British Library

Print Book ISBN: 978-1-80441-086-8
eBook ISBN: 978-1-80441-087-5

Acknowledgements

This research was funded by the Royal Institute of Chartered Surveyors (RICS). The conclusions herein are those of the author, and do not necessarily reflect the views of the RICS. The author would like to thank construction professionals and stakeholders for their insights, input, guidance, and access to project information throughout the development of this research. The author would also like to acknowledge the many people in the production of this book. The editorial team at Ethics Press has made a powerful impact on the presentation and layout of the book. For their efforts and others the author is grateful.

Contents

List of figures

List of tables

Table of cases

Preface

Construction disputes by their very nature are often complex, sometimes multi-party disputes, many of which are not suited to either adjudication or traditional form of litigation (these being potentially slow, expensive and divisive). The sheer complexity of construction disputes often leading to expensive, time-consuming and stressful paths being trodden through the traditional resolution terrain creates a compelling case for the introduction of alternative approaches within this adversarial industry. The construction industry has become increasingly aware of the substantial legal costs it burdens itself with as a consequence of its high incidence of disputes. Moreover, this expenditure, which globally represents a substantial sum each year, is by no means reflective of the hidden costs of disputes, such as the damage to reputations and commercial relationships; cost of time spent by executive personnel; and cost of lost business opportunities.

Adjudication in the UK has been popularised by the Latham report (Constructing the Team) and latterly the Egan report (rethinking construction). Initially sought as a method of dispute resolution procedure which was low cost, maintained cash flow and settled by an individual familiar with the industry it seemed like a perfect fit for the requirements. However, today's adjudications proceedings are moving far and away from the ambitious ideals that first attracted the UK government, as well as the construction industry in general. Today it is extremely unlikely for an adjudication proceeding not to be drafted and reviewed by a legal team, expert witnesses sought and a significant amount of fees being paid.

The author combines an academic background in Construction Law with over 25 years of industrial experience, helping a range of construction clients to resolve their disputes. Having worked in the construction industry for over 25 years, the author has seen the enthusiasm that was once there for adjudication begin to wane. More and more adjudications are being launched and the effort and expense being expended to defend claims is becoming more and more significant. The author's experience is mostly in large frameworks using NEC contract provisions and often as a result of adjudications, relationships becoming fractured and the long-term objectives of parties are being lost. This has brought about the author's interest to research the industry view of current dispute resolution practices as well as what alternatives are available.

Over recent years, governments and key players in commerce have emerged as advocates of mediation as a first-choice method of settling disputes. While accepting that Statutory Adjudication, Arbitration has long been one of the most commonly used forms of final dispute resolution for construction and engineering projects, the value of mediation has also been widely acknowledged worldwide, as evidenced by the number of jurisdictions in which the courts enforce obligations on parties to negotiate and adopt mediation to settle construction disputes prior to litigation. Notwithstanding the growing interest in mediation, one of the key trends within the dispute resolution arena is the adoption of multi-tiered procedures that combine arbitration with other forms of ADR, or through alternative methods of structuring the arbitration procedure, allowing it to be managed more effectively.

Recent surveys have also highlighted the development of dispute avoidance strategies, growth of statutory adjudication, the potential role of technology in mediation and arbitration, settlement of cross-border mediation agreements, transparency in the arbitration and mediation practitioner selection process, and the education of future ADR practitioners as among the developments that are likely to shape the evolution of dispute avoidance and alternative dispute resolution as they adapt to the increasing need for flexibility in the evolving construction and engineering dispute resolution landscape.

Alternative methods of dispute resolution such as negotiation, mediation, adjudication and arbitration have become more widely used in recent years and serve to promote a more collaborative approach to the resolve of disputes. With the use of alternative dispute resolution methods, both parties attempt to agree on a way forward and alleviate the necessity to facilitate costly court proceedings and undoubtedly damaging their relationship with the other side. There appears to be a general aura surrounding the power behind these alternative methods of dispute resolution, however, and their capacity to provide a solution to large scale cost disputes within the construction industry.

Introduction

The word 'alternative' immediately indicates that there are other ways of resolving disputes. The traditional method of resolving disputes is via litigation. The system in the UK courts is an adversarial one, which involves the parties engaging in a contest before an independent tribunal. This contest does not involve a search for the truth; it merely involves each side revealing enough of the truth to establish its case. The adversarial process, by its very nature, leads to conflict. In the business world, the process of dispute resolution can therefore sour existing commercial relationships. In an area of industry where the business community is small, the effects can be far-reaching.

The term 'alternative dispute resolution' may appear to be a modern term but it can be traced back to 1800 BCE when disputes were settled through ADR in many areas. The definition of ADR can differ in terms of its specific elements, but it is generally defined as the resolution of a dispute without the intervention of the courts (Main, 2005). Over time, three main categories of ADR have been identified, which are labelled as the three pillars of dispute resolution: negotiation, mediation and adjudication (Edwards, 1985).

The dispute resolution landscape

Disputes in the UK construction industry are common, with potentially huge sums at stake. Construction projects are highly complex and typically feature challenging deadlines and high demands on quality. During challenging financial times, it is common for contractors to submit tenders at low prices to secure the award of a project and to avoid potential insolvency. Such projects are often plagued with disputes and claims involving delays in requests for additional works on the part of employers. Whatever the basis of a dispute may be, it is almost certain that some type of dispute will arise in a construction contract. The construction industry is highly litigious and disputes can be costly, not merely in a financial sense but also in terms of the breakdown of otherwise profitable relationships due to the conflict. While arbitration and adjudication are commonly used in the construction sphere as dispute resolution tools, the adversarial nature of such processes may hold deleterious consequences for parties in terms of financial costs, delays, risks and loss of business.

It was not until the late 1980s that it was realised that conventional litigation for construction disputes was far too cumbersome and expensive. This caused alternative dispute resolution (ADR) to develop in the construction sector. Likewise, the courts have also proven eager to embrace ADR during the early stages of litigation proceedings, particularly when litigation costs will exceed the amount in dispute.

The reduced costs and time involved in ADR have prompted its increasing use as a primary method for resolving construction disputes. Parties to construction disputes prefer ADR because they perceive them to be more creative and focused on problem-solving when compared to litigation, which is based on the adversarial, rigid 'win-lose' outcome. Standard forms of construction contracts now typically feature adjudication provisions for the resolution of disputes. There are, however, conflicting reports on the success of ADR in the UK construction industry. Few industry participants appear to have had actual experiences of ADR and there is little empirical data on UK experiences.

References

Edwards, H.T., (1985). Alternative dispute resolution: Panacea or anathema. Harv. L. Rev., 99, p.668.

Main, T.O., (2005). ADR: the new equity. U. Cin. L. Rev., 74, p.329.

Chapter One: The Co-Optation of the Techniques and Language of Alternative Dispute Resolution

1.1. Introduction

Alternative Dispute Resolution (ADR) is a consensual process where the parties agree to come to a solution, which means that autonomy is a central characteristic of this category of dispute resolution processes (Tidwell, 1998). Tidwell identifies that

> *"mediation is predicated upon mediation's flexibility informality and consensuality opening up the full dimension of the problem facing the parties. Parties come to mediation because it is flexible and thus convenient. Mediation is used because it is not adversarial, but rather seeks to satisfy the needs of the presenting parties (Tidwell, 1998, 157)".*

The very nature of mediation and other ADR processes is that it is based upon a consensual process, which is outside of the judicial system (Rozdeiczer, 2006).

The problem with co-optation is that it is judicialising ADR processes through avenues such as mandatory mediation or adjunctive adjudication processes (Katz, 1993). The implication of this is that there is a framework in place that is no longer consensual in nature; rather, it is merely an extension of the coercive power of the judicial system. In the UK, there is arguably a system of co-optation through Civil Procedure Rules (CPR) and Family Procedure Rules (FPR), because instead of promoting consensual mediation and ADR processes they are coercing individuals to comply with an obligation to engage in ADR prior to entering the courts.

Thus, this chapter examines the content of the CPR and FPR to determine whether there is a process of co-optation is occurring within the English and Wales jurisdiction.

1.2. The nature of ADR processes

Prior to engaging with the CPR and FPR, it is necessary to identify the key characteristics of ADR. The primary characteristic of ADR is consensuality (i.e. the parties have to agree to engage in the ADR process) (Gorierly et al, 2002). For example, within mediation it is envisaged that there will be a transformative process, in order to ensure that the parties come to a workable solution that maintains an ongoing relationship (McEldowney, 2012). However, mediation has been identified as an effective and flexible system that can reduce the pressure on national court systems (Gorierly et al, 2002).

The result of this is that national legislatures are developing rules that "promote" or "require" an ADR process to be engaged with, which can be identified as a form of coercion.

There are arguments that the promise of empowerment and independence do not exist within ADR, because there is generally some form of coercive third party (i.e. mediator, adjudicator, legal counsel) (Spencer, 1996). This means that there will be little difference if there was a required mediation process, because it debunks the myth of a truly consensual process (Spencer, 1996).

The problem that arises is that there is a fundamental failure to fully consider the actual nature of mediation and other ADR processes when it is treated as a coercive process, because there is a more complex nature than just the choice to use ADR (i.e. when the parties are engaged in the ADR process there is a right for them to determine how the process is conducted and whether an amicable solution is present or enforcement of an award[1]). These factors highlight that ADR is a transformative process, which requires consensuality at different levels. Thus, it is necessary to ensure that there is a framework in place that enables the transformative nature of ADR to be promoted.

Baruch Busch and Folger identify that

> *"Transformative mediators allow and trust people to find their own way through the conflict – and even more important—find themselves and each other, discovering and revealing the strength and understanding within themselves" (Baruch & Folger, 2004, 83).*

To create this understanding there cannot be a judicial based process, because this increases the level of coercion and undermines the purpose of ADR (Mironi, 2014). The question that arises is whether promotion of mediation or ADR can be treated as coercion (Abel, 1982).

The concept of co-optation can be more closely related to a mandatory process, but are the CPR and FPR in English law just as coercive when they attempt to "persuade" individuals to engage with an ADR process.

Persuading individuals to engage in ADR processes through the judicial process can be deemed as co-optation, because the choice of the individual to engage in ADR will be undermined if there is some form of legal sanction if s/he fails to do so (Coy & Hedeen, 2005). The trend to judicialisation of ADR processes has been identified by Ryan. As Ryan (2000) argues the compelling of ADR through "the increasing judicialization of ADR represents its co-optation. However, in the context of judicially mandated ADR, the state's involvement argues strongly for - if not compels - prioritizing the protection of constitutional rights".

---

[1] Excluding Arbitration, because award enforcement is subject to national and international law principles.

The important factor highlighted is that if there is co-optation then there has to be increased safeguards put into place (i.e. constitutional/ human rights associated with due process). With the increased protections then the co-optation will be minimalized, although inevitably present (Ryan, 2000).

Therefore, this chapter will now turn to an examination of the potential co-optation of ADR processes and then move onto whether there are sufficient protections in place to prevent unfair coercion (i.e. human rights/constitutional processes). The focus of this discussion will be mediation, because it is the form of ADR where judicialisation is occurring in the UK.

1.3 The promotion of mediation

It has been identified that mediation is a transformative process, which is why it has been the focus of the CPR and FPR. For example, in family law mediation has been seen as the most effective process to engage in an amenable process between the parties (Norgrove, 2011;para 4.69). T*he Norgrove Report (Norgrove, 2011; para 4.69)* states:

> *"Our aim is a supportive, clear process for private law cases that promotes joint parental responsibility at all stages, provides information, manages expectations and that helps people to understand the costs they face. The emphasis throughout should be on enabling people to resolve their disputes safely outside court whenever possible" (Norgrove, 2011, para 4.69).*

The implication is that if there is a family dispute where there are children then there has to be an ongoing relationship (Cashmore & Parkinson, 2008). The use of the mediator and additional facilitators is important to ensure that the voice of the children is respected within the ADR process, which can be lost within the judicial framework (McEldowney, 2012).

The rationale is that through mediation there can be a better framework developed to create an ongoing amicable process, as opposed to the judicial system that is adversarial in nature (McEldowney, 2012). Thus, the ADR process (especially mediation) is seen as a better framework to protect vulnerable persons (as long as there is a specially trained mediator) (McEldowney, 2012).

The practice of mediation is not regulated in England and Wales, although many ADR organisations provide mediator qualifications through successful course completion or have their programmes accredited by Civil Mediation Council (Brooker 2011; 2013; Boon et al. 2007; Gould et al. 2010). While the EU Mediation Directive (Directive 2008 /52/EC) provides mediation should be used to settle cross border civil disputes (Cornes, 2008), this system has been criticised as being quasi-mandatory, which means that it can undermine the consensuality of the mediation process (Cornes, 2008). The text of the Mediation Directive does not use absolutist language, which can be seen in the text of Article 4(1):

> *"Member States shall encourage, by any means which they consider appropriate, the development of, and adherence to, voluntary codes of conduct by mediators and organisations providing mediation services, as well as other effective quality control mechanisms concerning the provision of mediation service"*[2].

The obligation of the state is the promotion of medication and not the enforcement of mediation. As Article 4(1) provides, there must be promotion of quality and appropriate mediation processes to enable an efficient and cost-effective regime[3].

---

[2] Article 4(1) Mediation Directive

[3] ibid, 38

1.4. Quality and appropriate mediation

The fact that the EU Mediation Directive indicates that there has to be a quality process highlights that mediation should only be required/ promoted when it is appropriate to the circumstances of the dispute (Greatbatch & Dingwall, 1999).

The question is whether this balance is being promoted within English law because the *Norgrove Report* states:

> *"It should become the norm that where parents need additional support to resolve disputes they would first attempt mediation or another dispute resolution service" (Norgrove, 2011, para 115).*

The inference is that there is a framework in place that is promoting mediation, but in such a way that there is a high degree of coercion (i.e. supporting the argument of co-optation). However, this would be incorrect to assume because the English Family Procedures Rules 2010 (FPR 2010) both support the principles that if mediation or ADR processes are engaged then the parties have to agree (and no sanctions will be imposed for reasonable rejection) (Blake et al, 2013).

Rule 3.2 of the FPR 2010 requires that the courts examine whether the ADR process is more appropriate than use of judicial processes.

This is supported by Rule 3.3 FPR 2010, which requires the courts to consider whether: (i) dispute resolution is appropriate in the given context[4]; (ii) there has been fair and proper information given in regards to the ADR process[5]; and (iii) the parties agree[6]. Within the

---

[4] Rule 3.3.1 FPR 2010

[5] Rule 3.3.1.a FPR 2010

[6] Rule 3.3.1.b FPR 2010

family law context there has to be examination of the context in detail, because if there is domestic abuse or a vulnerable child then there will be enhanced harm to the child (McEldowney, 2012) (or the party that has been subjected to domestic violence).

Article 4(2) of the Mediation Directive identifies that "Member States shall encourage the initial and further training of mediators in order to ensure that the mediation is conducted in an effective, impartial and competent way in relation to the parties".

This principle highlights that it is necessary for there to be quality mediation, which is paramount to ensure that there is not promotion of a process that may undermine justice because the circumstances belie any chance of consensuality due to the power relations that are involved. It is paramount to ensure that mediation retains the central characteristic of a "peace-seeking, transformative conflict resolving and human problem solving" (Genn, 2010) process. Nonetheless, there is an argument that if co-optation is to be the norm then it should not matter whether the parties agree or not.

1.5. The commercial realm

The interaction between court promoted ADR and the judicial process is more developed within the area of commercial law, because there is a greater deal of complexity due to the interaction between promoted ADR and chosen ADR.

A significant strand of Lord Woolf's plans for ADR was that courts should design Pre-action Protocols (PAPs) to deal with specific areas of litigation with the objective of emphasising the prompt settlement of disputes before legal action[7] (Woolf 1996; Brooker 2013; Gerber & Mailman, 2005).

---

[7] See CPR Pre-Action Conduct 1.1

One of the first cases in the Technology and Construction Court which illustrates how ADR is connected to litigation is *Paul Thomas Construction Ltd v Hyland* (2000), when a builder offered to use ADR with the homeowners but the court found he had made 'unreasonable' conditions over the payment of the neutral and indemnity costs were awarded for contravening court protocols by beginning proceedings without considering other methods of settlement (Brooker 2010; Gerber & Mailman, 2005).

Many TCC judges are renowned for their support of ADR and mediation is often recommended to the parties as a course of action (Brooker 2009; 2010(a); 2010(b); 2013; Brooker & Lavers 2002). For example, in *Brookfield Construction (UK) Ltd v Mott MacDonald Ltd* [2010] after two case management meetings with the parties Coulson J issued a vigorous warning to end their 'uncooperative' approach and to consider some type of ADR because the size of the dispute (combined claims of over £75 million) involving 'finance and documents' made it 'ideally suitable' for mediation and moreover both litigants were forewarned that a failure to mediate by one party would be considered in costs.

There are also some areas where it has been recognised that there has to be specialist training (such as housing law) due to the presence of a weaker party (i.e. the tenant and landlord; consumer and vendor) (Arden, 2013). The power imbalance may create a situation where any co-opted mediation would be unfair. In *Halsey v Milton Keynes NHS and Dunnett v Railtrack* such power imbalances were examined within the context of ADR processes. In the *Dunnet Case* the parties were a private individual and Railtrack where the former was willing to mediate, but the latter party did not, Railtrack won the case and made a claim for costs, the courts refused because Railtrack unreasonably refused to mediate (a better option in the case).

The implication is that the judiciary can promote mediation through sanctions for failing to engage in the process, even if it is in contradiction of the consensuality of the mediation process (Fisher et al, 1991). *Halsey v Milton Keynes NHS* also concerned a private individual and a large organisation (i.e. part of the NHS) where the large organisation refused to mediate.

The private individual lost who tried to avoid costs based upon *Dunnett v Railtrack*, but in this case the court refused, because there was not unreasonable refusal. The implication is that there is still a measure of choice within the mediation process, which means that there is minimized co-optation (i.e. the CPR prefer mediation, but there will be no sanctions when reasonably refused).

Thus, this counters the argument that mediation or ADR will be mandated. One route that may be taken is to have legal professionals consider whether it is relevant.

As Dyson LJ in *Burchell v Bullard* held:

> *"All members of the legal profession who conduct litigation should now routinely consider with their clients whether their disputes are suitable for ADR".*

This means that if the legal professional can provide evidence in the given circumstances that the mediation would be inappropriate then the courts will not impose cost sanctions. In other words, the courts have to assess the suitability of the mediation /ADR process to the particular dispute[8].

---

[8] Faidi & Anor v Elliot Corporation [2012] EWCA Civ 287

The main factor that the court will determine is whether in the given circumstances there is a chance of success[9]. Nonetheless, there is a presumption that when there are commercial parties with equal power that some form of mediation has been engaged with before using litigation[10].

1.6. Why cooptation in the commercial realm

The rationale for supporting judicial and legislative recommendations of using mediation and ADR processes is that if offers a more efficient and cost-effective system for the parties (and the courts are not clogged up with cases that could have been resolved otherwise)[11]. The reason for mediation and ADR processes being promoted in the commercial realm has been clearly espoused in *Aird v Prime Meridian Ltd*[12] where it was held that mediation is "a form of neutrally assisted negotiation"[13]. In this form of negotiation there is greater independence for the parties, because the process "need not necessarily be based on the underlying legal rights or obligations of the parties. Instead, the parties, with the assistance of the mediator, can reach a solution which is tailored to their real needs and interests"[14]. The inference is that mediation (and ADR processes) will be more capable of supporting the interests of the parties and coming to an amicable solution than objective and abstract judicial determination. Thus, this gives rise to the principle of co-optation within the CPR.

---

[9] PGF II SA v OMFS [2013] EWCA Civ 1288

[10] Charlton v Kenny [2010] EWCA Civ 873

[11] Lord Justice Jackson Review of Civil Litigation Costs Final Report (TSO, 2011) para 4.11

[12] Aird v Prime Meridian Ltd [2006] EWCA Civ. 1866

[13] ibid at 5

[14] ibid at 5

The primary reason for co-optation is to enable the courts to deal with cases justly[15], which is best achieved through limiting the burden of cases that reach the judicial system. This is supported by r. 1.1(2) CPR 1998, which provides that alternative processes should be used when practical.

The determination of practicality is based upon (a) equality; (b) saving expense; (c) proportionality in respect to the value of the claim, the importance of the case, complexity of the issues; and the financial position of each party; (d) assurance that the case is "dealt with expeditiously and fairly; and (e) allotting to it an appropriate share of the court's resources, while taking into account the need to allot resources to other cases"[16]. These factors will be examined by the courts, in order to promote mediation/ADR. However, it cannot force such processes on the parties.

Rather, it may merely indicate that there may be negative cost implications for the failure to consider a more appropriate alternative to the judicial process[17].

The latest amended Pre-Action Protocol for Construction and Engineering Disputes was published in 2014 and is applicable to 'all construction and engineering disputes (including professional negligence claims against architects, engineers and quantity surveyors).[18]. The TCC Protocol is the only one which requires the litigants to participate in a Pre-action Meeting before issuing proceeding where they have to discuss the issues between them and consider whether there are other methods of settling all or parts of the

[15] r. 1.1(1) CPR 1998
[16] r. 1.1(2) CPR 1998
[17] Practice Direction Protocols CPR 1998 r. 4.7
[18] This protocol can be used in other courts when the dispute relates to construction or engineering.

dispute (TCC Court Guide 2014, 2.4.3; Brooker 2010(a); 2013). Section 5.4 obliges litigants to deliberate on whether ADR would be more appropriate than court and if so to determine what type of dispute resolution process to use but also expressly states that 'no party' should be compelled to go to mediation or any other ADR procedure.

1.7. The limits of cooptation in the common law

There is a fundamental right for the parties to choose how they will access justice, in order to resolve a dispute (Quek, 2010). This is supported by the case of *Weissfisch v Julius*[19] where it was held that it is not possible for the courts to mandate ADR. Rather, it can only assess whether that have been any "efforts made, if any, before and during the Proceedings an order to try and resolve the dispute"[20] to determine whether there should be negative cost implications.

A mere refusal will not give rise to negative cost implications; rather the court has to determine whether the refusal is reasonable or not[21]. The application of negative cost implications is not considered to be a breach of consensuality or due process, because it is not an additional sanction; rather, it is a discretionary determination of how court costs will be divided[22].

Hickman v Blake Lapthorn and Another[23] held that:

> *"A party cannot be ordered to submit to mediation as that would be contrary to Article 6 of the European Convention on Human*

---

[19] Weissfisch v Julius [2006] EWCA Civ 218

[20] Dunnet v. Railtrack plc (in administration) [2002] EWCA Civ 303

[21] Halsey v Milton Keynes General NHS Trust [2004] EWCA Civ 576

[22] Charlton v Kenny [2010] EWCA Civ 873

[23] Hickman v Blake Lapthorn and Another [2006] EWHC 12 (QB)

Rights [and]... A party's reasonable belief that he has a strong case is relevant to the reasonableness of his refusal"[24].

The application of this case confirms the principle of consensuality where mandating mediation or ADR would be a breach of human rights (i.e. the process would be deemed unconstitutional because there is a lack of due process). Nonetheless, this does not prevent the promotion of ADR, which can include negative cost implications for wasting the court's time. One could argue that this is a case of mandated ADR; however, as long as the party shows that the decision not to engage in an ADR process is reasonable there will be no cost sanctions. Therefore, the main factor that the English CPR rules have developed is balance, in order to promote more individuals (when appropriate) to engage with ADR processes. This is still a form of co-optation, but there are safeguards and limits to protect the parties that are engaging in the process.

1.8. Summary

The move towards mediation in England and Wales was as a direct result of Lord Woolf's recommendations to reform the legal system were implemented by the Civil Procedure Act 1997 and the Civil Procedure Rules 1999. The key overriding objective was set out in Rule 1.1 as "enabling the court to deal with cases justly". Parties are obliged to achieve this objective by clearly setting out the issues in dispute, identifying key documents, and, in particular, attempting to avoid litigation by settling the dispute.

The courts have acknowledged the importance of ADR. The Civil Procedure Rules (CPR), governing court procedures, encourages the

[24] Ibid at 18

use of alternate dispute resolution methods, prior to litigation, in order to avoid going to trial with its inherent cost. Questions over the extent to which the courts may encourage or even compel parties to consider ADR, and how the courts should deal with a party that refuses to engage in ADR, have been the subject of much case law and commentary over the years.

The case law within England and Wales also emphasises that the court is ready and willing to enforce ADR clauses contained in construction contracts. An issue which has dominated deliberations in the Technology and Construction Courts (TCCs) in recent years is whether parties which had declined to mediate may be sanctioned. The TCCs have distinguished between the situations where mediation was ordered by a court and cases in which mediation was suggested by the party that was unsuccessful in litigation. The prevailing sentiment is that the courts will encourage, indeed may strongly encourage, ADR but cannot compel its use.

References

Abel, RL (1982) The contradictions of informal justice. In: R.L. Abel, ed., The Politics of Informal Justice. Volume 1. The American Experience. (Academic Press), pp. 267-320, 268

Agapiou, A (2016) The co-optation of the techniques and language of alternative dispute resolution: a critical assessment of developments in the UK, International Journal of Arbitration, Mediation and Dispute Management, vol.82, issue 2, p129-134; ISSN: 0003-7877

Arden, A (2013) "A Plea for a Housing Mediation Service" (2013) Journal of Housing Law 57, 57

Baruch Bush, RA & Folger, JP (2004) The Promise of Mediation: The Transformative Approach to Mediation (Revised Ed, Josey-Bass, 2004), 83

Blake S, J Browne, & S Sime (2013) The Jackson ADR Handbook (Oxford University Press, 2013), 13.02

Boon A, Earle R & Whyte A (2007) Regulating mediators? Legal Ethics 10(1), 26

Brad Reich J (2002) Attorney v. client: creating a mechanism to address competing process, Southern Illinois University Law Journal Vol. 26, 183

Brooker P (2009) Criteria for the Appropriate Use of Mediation in Construction Disputes: Judicial Statements in the English Technology and Construction Court International Journal of Law in the Built Environment, Vol. 1 Issue 1, 82

Brooker P (2010a) Mediation in the UK Construction Industry in Brooker P and Wilkinson S (2010) (ed) Mediation in the Construction Industry: An International Review Spon Press imprint of Taylor and Francis Group.

Brooker P (2010b) Judging Unreasonable Litigation Behavior at the Interface of Mediation in the English Jurisdiction. Journal of Legal Affairs and Dispute Resolution in Engineering and Construction Vol. 2, No. 3, August, 2010, 148-161

Brooker P (2011) Towards a code of professional conduct for construction mediators, International Journal of Law in the Built Environment Vol. 3 Issue 1, 24

Brooker, P., (2013). Mediation law: Journey through institutionalism to juridification. Routledge.

Brooker P & Lavers A (2002) Commercial Lawyers' Attitudes and Experience with ADR 4 Web Journal of Current Affairs

Cashmore, J & Parkinson, P (2008) "Children's and Parent's Perceptions on Children's Participation in Decision Making after Parental Separation and Divorce" Family Court Review 46(91), 92

Cornes, D (2008) "Mediation Privilege and the EU Mediation Directive: An Opportunity". Arbitration 74(4), 395

Coy, P. and Hedeen, T (2005) 'A Stage Model of Social Movement Co-optation: Community Mediation in the United States'. The Sociological Quarterly 46(405), 410

Fisher, R., Patton, B. and Ury, W (1991) Getting to Yes: Negotiating Agreements without giving in, (Random House), 23

G Genn H (2010) Judging Civil Justice (CUP), 81

Gerber P and Mailman B (2005) Construction Litigation: Can we do it better, Monash University Law Review 31, 2, 237 Goriely, T, Moorhead, R and Abrams, P More (2002) Civil Justice? The Impact of the Woolf Reforms on Pre-Action Behaviour. Law Society and Civil Justice Council Research Paper 43, 2

Gould N, King C and Britton P (2010) Mediating Construction Disputes: An Evaluation of Existing Practice, Kings College London, Centre of Construction Law and Dispute Resolution, London

Greatbatch, D & Dingwall, R (1999) "The Marginalization of Domestic Violence in Divorce Mediation" (1999) International Journal of Law Policy and the Family 13(174), 176

Katz, LV (1993) Compulsory Alternative Dispute Resolution and Voluntarism: Two-Headed Monster or Two Sides of the Coin?" Journal of Dispute Resolution 1, 2

McEldowney, J (2012) Family Mediation in a Time of Change. FMC Review Final Report, 1

Mironi, M (2014) 'Mediation v. Case Settlement: The Unsettling Relations between Courts and Mediation' (2014) Harvard Negotiation Law Review 19(173), 177

Norgrove Report (2011) (Family Justice Review) November.

Quek, D (2010) "Mandatory Mediation: An Oxymoron?" (2010) 11(479) Cardozo J Conflict Resol, 479, 482.

Rozdeiczer, L (2006) ADR Manual. The World Bank Group. IFC. 1

Ryan, E (2000) "ADR, the Judiciary and Justice: Coming to Terms with the Alternatives" (2000) Harvard Law Review 1851, 1871

Spencer, D (1996) 'Exploding the Empowerment Myth of Alternative Dispute Resolution' Commercial Dispute Resolution 3(13), 15

TCC Court Guide (2014) 3rd Revision http://www.justice.gov.uk/downloads/courts/tech-court/tec-con-court-guide.pdf

Tidwell, A (1998) Conflict Resolved: A Critical assessment of Conflict Resolution. Continuum, 157

Woolf (1996) (The Right Honourable The Lord Wolf, Master of the Rolls) Access to Justice: The Final Report London: HMSO

Case Law

Aird v Prime Meridian Ltd [2006] EWCA Civ. 1866

Brookfield Construction (UK) Ltd v Mott MacDonald Ltd. [2010] EWHC (TCC) 659, 52-55

Burchell v Bullard [2005] EWCA Civ 358

Charlton v Kenny [2010] EWCA Civ 873

Dunnett v Railtrack [2002] EWCA Civ 302

Dunnet v. Railtrack plc (in administration) [2002] EWCA Civ 303

Faidi & Anor v Elliot Corporation [2012] EWCA Civ 287

Halsey v Milton Keynes General NHS Trust [2004] EWCA Civ 576

Hickman v Blake Lapthorn and Another [2006] EWHC 12 (QB)

PGF II SA v OMFS [2013] EWCA Civ 1288

Paul Thomas Construction Ltd v Hyland (2000) Adj. L. R 03/08

Weissfisch v Julius [2006] EWCA Civ 218

Chapter Two: The Reform of Civil Justice Procedures in England & Scotland

2.1 Introduction

This chapter reviews how the Civil Procedure Rules (CPR) have developed the use of ADR in England and Wales and how this is fulfilling a part of the Government's strategy which is to improve access to justice while at the same time reducing the cost of litigation for the public purse. The chapter will also exam how the courts in England and Wales have responded to the Civil Procedure Rules, and how this facilitated the growth of alternative methods of dispute disposal The chapter will consider what is being done in Scotland to achieve the Government objective and how the Scottish courts have not embraced ADR but instead have looked at reform of their procedures and case management as their contribution to providing a more effective system that provides better access to justice.

2.2. The need for reform

Lord Woolf produced an interim and final report on "Access to Justice" in England and Wales. The reports in 1995 and 1996 were part of a three-strand approach by the Government to the reform of the civil justice system of England and Wales. Lord Woolf looked at procedural reform leaving others to consider the two remaining strands being, reform of the Legal Aid System and an extension of the Conditional Fee Arrangement.

The objective of reforming Legal Aid for civil cases was to reduce the bill for Government by limiting the number of cases eligible for Legal Aid. It is arguable that this action contributed to the development of ADR, it being a lower cost option.

The Government was seeking to provide Legal Aid only in situations of public interest, social welfare needs and/or for judicial review. They had the expectation that insurance schemes, pro bono and/or contingent legal representation would grow to meet the needs of those able to fund or negotiate those measures. Over and above that the Government, by improving information resources, expected the public to develop better knowledge of their rights and obligations such that there would be fewer disputes and that the bulk of disputes remaining would be settled outwith the court. One method of achieving this aim was greater use of ADR.

The actions of the Government were an understandable response to the system pertaining at the time of Woolf's interim report. He identified the primary problems as;

> *"the excesses of and the lack of control over the system of civil litigation; the inadequate attention which the system gives to the control of costs and delay and to the need to ensure equality between the parties; the complexity of the present system; and the absence of any satisfactory judicial responsibility for the effective use of resources within the civil system."*[25]

His views then centred on changes to case management for civil litigation, placing greater responsibility with the courts and reducing and restructuring the input of the parties and their legal advisors.

He saw ADR making a significant contribution to avoiding, or reducing the extent of, proceedings in court;

"The parties should:

[25] Ch. 4 Access to Justice: Interim Report to the Lord Chancellor on the Civil Justice System of England and Wales (1995)

whenever it is reasonable for them to do so settle their disputes (either the whole dispute or individual issues comprised in the dispute) before resorting to the courts; where it is not possible to resolve a dispute or an issue prior to proceedings, then they should do so at as early a stage in the proceedings as is possible. Where there exists an appropriate alternative dispute resolution mechanism which is capable of resolving a dispute more economically and efficiently than court proceedings, then the parties should be encouraged not to commence or pursue proceedings in court until after they have made use of that mechanism."[26]

He also looked at extending small claims jurisdiction to £3000 and introducing a summary procedure for claims up to £10,000. Under his proposals the courts would be more interventionist and pro-active at managing the flow of litigation.

In Chapter 1 paragraph 16 of his Final Report, Lord Woolf stated the "Essential elements" of his proposals for case management that confirmed his support for greater use of ADR;

"16. Essential elements of my proposals for case management include:

...encouraging and assisting the parties to settle cases or, at least, to agree on particular issues; encouraging the use of ADR;.."[27]

In forming these proposals Lord Woolf had looked at both international approaches to case management and also a number of schemes in the UK that were either in operation prior to commencement of his review or that had started in parallel with it.

---

[26] ibid

[27] Ch. 1, para 16 *Access to Justice: Final Report to the Lord Chancellor on the Civil Justice System of England and Wales* (1996).

Among these he endorsed the view expressed in the Practice statement of the Commercial Court dated 10 December 1993 "*...that it is right that the court should encourage the parties to consider the use of ADR as a means of resolving their disputes.*"[28]

He also looked at the Ancillary Relief Pilot Scheme (Family Courts) (1996) that underwent trials in 28 courts in England and Wales[29]. This, inter alia, required the district judge to refer the case to a Financial Dispute Resolution (FDR) appointment, unless he decided, exceptionally, that such a referral was not appropriate. The FDR meeting would take place before another district judge who carried out a mediation process with evaluation, the objective being settlement at that stage.

The best example he found to look to in the UK was the pilot scheme that operated in the Central London County Court that had started in 1996. The court operated a court-annexed mediation scheme that was the subject of a detailed report by Professor Hazel Genn of the Law Faculty of University College London [30].

Her findings showed that, while take-up of the voluntary scheme was low (around 5%), which she felt reflected widespread ignorance of and opposition to the procedure, the majority of mediations that took place settled at the mediation (62%).

She also found that cases that had not settled at the time still had a much higher settlement rate further downstream than those that had not gone to mediation.

---

[28] para 7(d), ibid.

[29] Rules 2.71 to 2.77 of the Family Proceedings Rules 1991 contain the procedure for the Pilot Scheme.

[30] Research Papers 1997, No. 5/98 the Central London County Court Pilot Mediation Scheme – Evaluation Report.

It was also the perception of 77% of those that had settled at mediation that the mediation had shortened the period to settlement with even those going on to litigation being broadly evenly balanced regarding the time impact of the mediation. 32% thought it had saved time and 36% thought it had added time to settlement.

Her research showed that in commercial disputes, parties in mediation preferred an evaluative rather than a facilitative third party. This particular finding could be used to develop the use of ADR in commercial disputes and will be considered for that purpose later in this document.

Another finding was that under the present system the costs of litigation were generally as much as the sum sought. This finding applied up to a claim value of around £50,000 if the costs to both parties were considered, but not court costs as that would increase even further the imbalance between sum claimed to cost of recovery.

Lord Woolf took on board all these findings in preparing his final report that led to the introduction of the new Civil Procedure Rules in 1999.

Before moving on to consider the new rules it is worth noting some of the criticisms of Lord Woolf's reforms that were made at the time by various commentators.

Would the reforms provide the prospect of greater access to justice? Would they lead to a reduction in the number of disputes going through the courts?

Case management may in fact be a double-edged sword. On one hand the controls did offer the prospect of streamlining the previous procedures and also of identifying, at an early date, the most appropriate forum to deal with a dispute. On the other, some commentators anticipated that in order to provide the appropriate documents to allow effective case management to take place at an early stage, the parties themselves would need to be much more advanced with their preparation than was previously the case. The commitment needed to carry out that preparation meant that significant expense would arise at this early stage, which may provide greater impetus to continue the dispute process and at the least raise the stakes with respect to the settlement sum.

The better understanding of the issues by all concerned may again have further polarised the parties, in that if one or other of the parties, through greater knowledge, became more sanguine of his prospects of success, he was likely to be less inclined to enter a more conciliatory process and seek to remain in the adversarial stream.

The converse being that a loss of confidence in his prospects may have led to him "taking a punt" on ADR rather than abandon the case or reduce his level of expectation of a settlement sum at least at the outset of the procedure.

The overall effect on court time for disputes may in practice prove to be minimal. Fewer disputes of a marginal nature being advanced down the procedural stream but more disputes being identified earlier as being worth advancing and so removing them from a settlement/ compromise pool that they may have remained in previously.

Similarly, access to justice may not be improved. Lord Woolf identified that, under the existing procedures, access to justice had become restricted to those on Legal Aid and those who had sufficient resources to meet the substantial costs in the process up to settlement or judgement.

The new rules offered the prospect of lower costs downstream once a case was in the court system. However the entry level preparation costs, combined with constriction of those eligible for Legal Aid might in fact reduce the number of parties who were able to advance a legitimate dispute to the stage where case management took place. Accompanying developments in the conditional/contingency feeing system may help to offset these effects.

Another point to be considered was that if Government funding for "Justice" was taken as a single pot then the court systems needs for more administrators, better IT and more "judicial managers" may remove resource from the support of disputants.

This theme was indirectly referred to by Menkel-Meadow in his critique of Lord Woolf's Interim Report[31]. He referred to the legal economist, George Priest who argued that less delay in the process removed an incentive to settle so more cases would go to trial. More cases in the system would lead to new delays that would in turn lead to more settlement thus equilibrium would be maintained. However the equilibrium point would have moved up the scale in terms of case numbers. The mechanism for achieving the new equilibrium point was in fact through the spread across ADR procedures combined with further, probably more abbreviated, court procedures. All of this being contingent on the new resource level for administration.

So in effect the equation is if you spend more money you get more justice. This does not appear to sit well with the Government's objective of reducing expenditure.

---

[31] Achieving Civil Justice: Appropriate Dispute Resolution for the 1990's – R Smith (ed) (1996) Legal Action Group, London, pp 94-100.

2.3. The civil procedure rules for England and Wales 1999

The new Civil Procedure Rules for England and Wales became law on 26 April 1999. They included a number of references to ADR.

Rule 1 included reference to active case management and identified ADR as a part of that process

"Rule 1.4(2) Active case management includes –

(a)…
encouraging the parties to use an alternative dispute resolution procedure if the court considers that appropriate and facilitating the use of such a procedure;…"

Rule 26.4 introduced the conditions for attempting ADR. It allowed proceedings to be stayed for one month, or longer at the discretion of the judge, at the preliminary stage while ADR was tried as a vehicle to settlement.

"Rule 26.4

A party may, when filing the completed allocation questionnaire, make a written request for the proceedings to be stayed while the parties try to settle the dispute by alternative dispute resolution or other means.

Where –

all parties request a stay under paragraph (1); or
the court of its own initiative, considers that such a stay would be appropriate, the court will direct that the proceedings be stayed for one month."

The ADR procedure was optional at the election of at least one of the parties to the dispute. There was no compulsion at this stage and, possibly more significantly, no opportunity for introduction of ADR at a later stage of the litigation procedure.

This latter point is a criticism of the wording of the clause as a later stay during the process could, in the particular circumstances, be productive in reaching settlement where the early procedure may have failed. As the case unfolds, both parties could have developed better appreciation of their relative positions, making them more inclined to focus on settlement. While the Rules do not accommodate a later stay, thus there is no specific vehicle for the Judge to promote such an intervention, nevertheless the parties would be free to act off-stage if they thought that ADR was appropriate.

Rule 44.3 dealt with the court's discretion, and circumstances to be considered, when exercising its options with respect to costs. It gives the court ample room to respond to the approaches of the parties and to penalise them where they do not take the opportunity to avoid, or minimise the scope of, the litigation.

"44.3 (1) The court has discretion as to -

(a) whether costs are payable by one party to another;
(b) the amount of those costs; and
(c) when they are to be paid.

(4) In deciding what order (if any) to make about costs, the court must have regard to all the circumstances, including -

(a) the conduct of all the parties;

(5) The conduct of the parties includes –

(a) conduct before, as well as during, the proceedings and in particular the extent to which the parties followed any relevant pre-action protocol;
(b) whether it was reasonable for a party to raise, pursue or contest a particular allegation or issue;
(c) the manner in which a party has pursued or defended his case or a particular allegation or issue;..."

Rule 44.5 addressed the factors to be taken into account when deciding the amount and allocation of costs. Again the court has wide discretion, taking all things into account, whether costs attributable are proportionate and reasonable thus allowing them to impose the cost sanction to the extent they see fit.

"44.5 (1) The court is to have regard to all the circumstances in deciding whether costs were –

(a) if it is assessing costs on the standard basis –

(i) proportionately and reasonably incurred; or
(ii) were proportionate and reasonable in amount, or

(b) if it is assessing costs on the indemnity basis –

(i) unreasonably incurred; or
(ii) unreasonable in amount."

The new rules objective as stated in Rule 1.1 were designed for "enabling the Court to deal with cases justly" and in doing so they sought to be as inclusive as possible of the range of options by which closure and/or settlement could be reached. They were sufficiently open to allow a fairly broad interpretation by the presiding neutral of the procedure and the commitment of the parties to reach settlement. The neutral could respond to this commitment, or lack of it, when attributing costs for the procedure and this sanction gave the court an opportunity to support ADR by penalising parties who could have, and should have, gone down that route.

2.4. ADR following the civil procedure rules

The new Civil Procedure Rules were intended to give impetus to the use of ADR as a significant means of resolving disputes and in particular of giving parties an option prior to, or even during, the litigation process.

Over the period since their introduction the Government has promoted ADR as part of their strategy of providing better access to justice and as a tool to dissipate conflict and focus the minds of parties in dispute on settlement.

As well as issuing information on ADR through the Lord Chancellor's Department, among others, they have also sought to measure reaction to their ADR strategy.

In 1999 the Lord Chancellor's Department issued a discussion paper on Alternative Dispute Resolution to explain their views of ADR and its delivery as a service. The document was titled simply "Alternative Dispute Resolution – A Discussion Paper"[32]. They raised various open questions in the paper and sought the recipients' responses to build their knowledge of how the key influencers on the procedure were reacting to it.

Around 3000 copies of the paper and integral survey were sent to solicitors, barristers, the Law Society and other legal bodies, ADR

[32] Lord Chancellor's Department – November 1999

organisations and providers and bodies involved in dispute resolution as a core element of their operation e.g. the Trades Union Congress and the National Consumer Council. One-hundred and thirty three responses were received and these were recorded in a separate response document.

2.4.1. The discussion paper

The document's introduction outlined the Government's intent to resolve legal problems outside the court system[34], to improve "Access to Justice"[35], to settle disputes at the earliest possible stage[36] and to replace the Legal Aid Board with the Legal Service Commission. The Legal Service Commission would then replace Civil Legal Aid with the Community Legal Service Fund[37]. It was proposed that the new provision would provide funding for ADR at the expense of support for litigation. Sections 1.12 and 1.13 of the introduction noted that take-up of ADR schemes was very low, Professor Genn placed it at around 5%, and the Government was looking for reasons such that ADR could be used more effectively.

Over the remainder of the paper, they set out the arguments for and against the use of ADR. They made the point that a better description of ADR might have been "appropriate dispute resolution"[38] (the description was picked up by a number of the respondents as a more useful description.[39] Other commentators on ADR have also agreed

[33] ADR Discussion Paper: Summary of Responses

[34] Clause 1.1

[35] Clause 1.3

[36] Clause 1.4

[37] Clause 1.5

[38] Clause 2.5 See also *The ADR Practice Guide – Commercial Dispute Resolution by Mackie, Miles, Marsh and Allen (2000)* p9 "…'Appropriate' or 'Additional' (in the sense of complementary) Dispute Resolution…"

[39] Para 5, Summary of Responses

this description is better but they recognise that "alternative" has entered common parlance). They presented the argument that the less formal setting and procedure for ADR reduced stress and was more conducive to continuing relationships.

Around 51% of the respondents found ADR beneficial in terms of speed and time although a few pointed out that arbitration was at least as expensive as litigation. 67% of respondents agreed that ADR provided other benefits to the parties with 34% referring to the preservation or rebuilding of relationships as the most significant of these.

In response to a question on the drawbacks of ADR, it was generally accepted that there was more in favour of ADR than against it. However, one point was made that mediators could bring inappropriate emotional pressure to bear when trying to reach settlement with one lawyer comparing the techniques of mediators "to those of double glazing salesmen."[40]

They referred to Professor Genn's research in the Central London County Court, see earlier references, and in particular identified the "imbalance of power"[41] as a possible factor against mediation. The research did not appear to make much of this point but it could, in the longer term, prove to be very significant.

Various issues need to be explored further in this regard;

The neutral is not a judge and is likely to be dependent on private clients for continuing business. The relative commercial strength of the parties could mean one may have been in the past, or is potentially

---

[40] Para 11, ibid.

[41] Clause 4.9

in the future, a source of business. This could affect the confidence of the other party to the dispute that he has the prospect of an equitable solution. The issue does not arise in the courts where the judge would exercise his own experience and skill to protect the weaker party from oppression.

The strength of the opposing team, its experience and its level of preparation may put it at an advantage against an inexperienced opponent and possibly a less experienced neutral than themselves. There is an opportunity to spin matters out even further than in the traditional litigation by a less than sincere approach to the process. Thus the injured party becomes weakened further commercially before any litigation.

The foregoing factors present a challenge to the ADR process and the neutrals in particular and it may be that ADR can work best in situations where the parties feel they are equally matched and their interests are focused on solving "the problem".

Genevieve Chornenki in her article "Mediating Commercial Disputes: Exchanging "Power Over" for "Power With"[42] took the view that the Mediator's skills could be exercised to redress any imbalance of power;

> *"To strike the balance, the mediator provides the necessary power underpinnings to the weaker negotiator – information, advice, friendship – or reduces those of the stronger. If he cannot balance the power relationship, the mediator can bargain with or use his power against the stronger negotiator to constrain the exercise of his power."*[43]

---

[42] Rethinking Disputes: The Mediation Alternative (1997) pp 163-168, J Macfarlane (ed)

[43] ibid

This of course relies upon the skill and experience of the neutral, as noted above, and his ability to take a more interventionist role that would, to some degree, be alien to a facilitative role, if that was his terms of engagement. The neutral in these circumstances would be required to proactively manage the process. Only a small percentage of the respondents thought the mediator could redress imbalance of power, the majority of those holding that view were involved in mediation.

The over-riding principle that the procedure was a voluntary one, that the parties were entering the process in good faith and that their objective was to reach an agreed settlement, to a large extent, overcame the reservations expressed above. There was no compulsion for the parties to settle unless it was in their interest to do so.

There was about a 40% response to a question on the criteria for assessing the suitability of ADR. The two criteria getting greatest support were; the cost of the process in relation to the claim value and the willingness of the parties to try ADR. Another interesting response was regarding the development of a checklist to identify the appropriate ADR method. This garnered a mixed response with around 30% thinking a checklist would be useful and 25% against it. The question was clearly aimed at the more user friendly and simpler approach to entry planned by the Government but the responses showed the ambiguity in the field, where a general lack of experience may have been inhibiting too prescriptive an approach. It was significant that around 45% did not express a view.

Sections 5 and 6 of the paper considered how the awareness of ADR could be raised, referring to the new Community Legal Service as providing "greater cohesion"[44] to the process.

---

[44] Clause 5.3

It also referred to the public information booklet "Resolving Disputes Without Going to Court" published in 1995 and distributed through various Government Agencies as a tool to raise potential client's awareness of the options. 56% of respondents thought that the booklet should be updated and distributed widely.

The general lack of awareness among both service users and the suppliers, in particular lawyers, was seen as a significant obstacle to wider use of ADR. The paper raised various questions about the methods of improving awareness. The strong theme in responses was education both through professional training and a more general raising of awareness through the media. 64% responded to the question on the production of an ADR directory. The overwhelming majority agreed that a directory of ADR providers would contribute to the promotion of ADR.

The commitment of the Government was seen as a key component in the development of ADR as an alternative to litigation. The inclusion of ADR clauses in Government contracts would provide a clear lead. Further development of the court-annexed ADR schemes was seen as another device to aid development, although the possibility of extending trials to a national level received a lukewarm reception. A form of Legal Aid for ADR was also seen as a means of increasing its use.

On the question of delivery, the bulk of respondents agreed that a set service for a fixed fee would be an incentive to adoption of ADR. Value for money and a better understanding of how the investment to return equation worked out were a part of this response which again may point towards the general lack of knowledge of ADR. A fixed sum would allow a better appreciation of the risk in adopting the procedure.

Another tool to encourage use received 50% of the respondents' support in that they thought Pre-action protocols should require consideration of ADR. These Pre-action protocols would bring ADR into a very early stage of a case and so the issue would be broached before preparation had reached the point of being ready for litigation. Thus genuine savings might be made if the decision to employ ADR was made at that time.

55 of 66 respondents thought ADR should be available to the parties throughout the whole case flow. This measure would extend the role for ADR included in the new Rules. A formal reference would give the action procedural integrity and would allow the offer to be made by the court. However the question that arose was, if the parties, who would be free to get together to seek a pause in the formal process to attempt a compromise by whatever means, did not see this as a way ahead for themselves, would they respond to overtures by the court?

It could be argued that the added option of this pointer by the court might break deadlock in the parties strategic thinking and may also be seen as a way for the parties to step away from the litigation with neither being "seen to blink". In any case if the option was to be available it could only help to develop the overall employment of ADR as a vehicle for resolving disputes.

The question of compulsion in the use of ADR was addressed in section 7 of the paper. The leading view was that it should be a voluntary procedure and many of the respondents drew attention to the European Convention of Human Rights, in particular Article 6 regarding the right of a party to a fair and public hearing, prohibiting compulsion of such a procedure. Compulsion was in effect also considered under the question regarding an opt-out or opt-in clause for ADR. The respondents were split 50% to 50% in favour of each option. More ADR specialists favoured opt-out whereas more lawyers saw this verging towards compulsion and so favoured opt-in schemes. 46% of respondents to the paper did not express an opinion on the question which, when taken with the ECHR point, would probably suggest opt-out, a more radical step, was a non-starter at this time.

Sanctions for unreasonably refusing to try ADR were also covered in section 7. 34% were in favour with 25% against although, as sanctions in effect required a positive response, it could be suggested that the remaining 41% who didn't reply could not be said to be strongly disposed towards the application of sanctions. Going on from there, the question of whether sanctions should be applied for acting unreasonably in an ADR procedure was asked. A majority of respondents (44) agreed there should be cost sanctions for acting unreasonably. However some respondents sought a clear definition of what would constitute unreasonable behaviour and a number did not consider delay sufficient to fit this description even though an essential element of ADR is that it speeds up the process of getting to settlement.

Of 75 respondents, 74 were in favour of preserving the confidentiality of the ADR process. The strength of feeling on that point is an indicator of one of the advantages of a settlement reached by ADR.

Section 8 of the paper dealt with quality control of ADR procedures and how the third-party neutrals and the various schemes could be regulated.

57% of respondents were in favour of a code of practice for mediators (the question read "mediators" as opposed to ADR practitioners). The lack of a defined standard may itself be a cause for the limited adoption of ADR procedures by lawyers who have to meet professional standards and may be uncomfortable at allowing an unregulated and informal grouping of practitioners to have an influential role in resolving disputes away from the traditional litigation path.

By way of addressing this particular concern, CEDR (the Centre for Effective Dispute Resolution) and other recognised bodies in the field of ADR have established the Joint Mediation Forum to create a code of conduct for mediators. They have also been working towards forming a regulating body for the ADR "profession". CEDR have published a number of "model form" agreements.

These include an ADR code of conduct[45], contract clauses for an ADR agreement[46], a mediation agreement[47] now up to its 8th Edition, an early neutral evaluation agreement[48], an expert determination agreement[49], an executive tribunal procedure[50] and a settlement agreement[51]. Each of these "model form" agreements have been designed to simplify and to help to regulate ADR procedures. There is no compulsion to adopt the forms available, indeed CEDR has recognised that they require to be adapted to the ADR situation;

"This document contains a 'menu' of ADR contract clauses, with particular focus on mediation, which can be used individually or linked into 'multi-step' dispute resolution provisions. The clauses are only model clauses and will need to be selected for, and adapted to, the circumstances and legal requirements of the particular contract."[52]

However the production of the forms provides a convenient menu for ADR practitioners and for those instructing them it gives a recognised structure and form to the various ADR procedures. In turn, that would allow the parameters, for the parties and their relationship

---

[45] Code of Conduct for mediators and other third-party neutrals, CEDR 2001

[46] Model Contract Clauses - Fast track drafting guide to key dispute resolution clauses, CEDR 2001

[47] Model Mediation Procedure & Agreement 8th Edition October 2002

[48] Model Early Neutral Evaluation Agreement including guidance notes, CEDR 2001

[49] Model Expert Determination Agreement including guidance notes, CEDR 2001

[50] Model Executive Tribunal Procedure including guidance notes, CEDR 2001

[51] Model Settlement Agreement & Tomlin Order, CEDR 2001

[52] Model ADR Contract Clauses – How and why, Model Contract Clauses, CEDR 2001

to the neutral third party, to be defined and monitored during the procedure. A level of regulation was thus available for the conduct of the procedure and for the settlement agreement.

The paper recorded the start of these developments although the forms produced by CEDR dated from 2001. The developments by CEDR and the other ADR groups provide a response to the concerns of the respondents to questions regarding systems of approval for ADR schemes and practitioners.

The conclusions drawn in the discussion paper were that the Government, while seeking to include ADR as part of the dispute resolution menu, recognised that ADR was still, in November 1999, at a formative stage and the most effective means of promoting its use remained to be decided.

Probably the most interesting statistic to note on the discussion paper and its responses was that there were only 133 responses to the 3000 papers distributed giving a 4.4% return. While this was, in itself, fairly consistent of surveys in general, it was still a very small sample to allow any definitive conclusions to be drawn from it.

In June 2000 the Lord Chancellor's Department issued a strategy paper titled "civil.justice.2000" that followed an earlier consultation paper "Civil.Justice: Resolving and Avoiding Disputes in the Information Age". The purpose of the strategy paper was to define the Government's vision of the civil justice system in the near future. The paper was partly a statement of intent and partly a crystal ball gazing exercise to show what the future of civil justice might look like.

2.4.2. Civil.Justice.2000

There were four parts to the strategy vision. The first two parts addressed increasing citizen's awareness and understanding of their rights and obligations. The latter two parts established the role of ADR;

"Our vision is of a civil justice system which:

...encourages the avoidance and early resolution of disputes ....helps ensure that the most appropriate form of dispute resolution is selected"[53]

The paper referred to the role that IT had in fulfilling the Government's strategy that included the launch of a Government search engine site called "Just Ask!"[54].

In setting out the planks of the strategy in an executive summary, the paper stated;

"Our current view of the civil justice system is litigation and court based. We believe that we should want much more than an effective court system in the future.

We should want an integrated civil justice system wherein the courts are a forum of last resort."[55]

It then went on to show a flow chart representing the Government's vision of an integrated Civil Justice System which was in four key parts that represented information and education of the public being prerequisites to the future of resolving disputes.

---

[53] civil.justice.2000 Preface by David Lock MP, Parliamentary Secretary, Lord Chancellor's Department

[54] www.justask.org.uk

[55] Clause 1.3 Ibid

Figure 2.1. *The Government's vision of an integrated civil justice system*

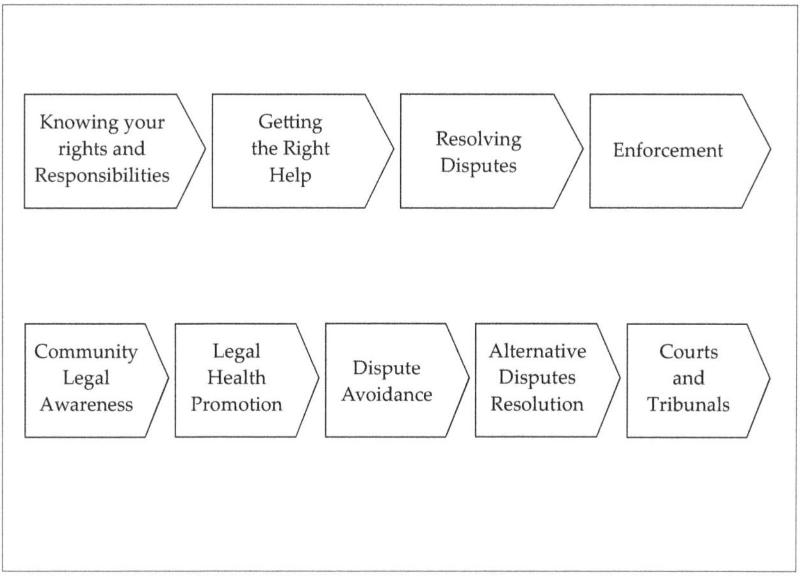

The flow chart showed that dispute avoidance was a primary aspect of their vision with the resolution of disputes taking place in two distinct stages. Firstly by Alternative Dispute Resolution and secondly by Courts and Tribunals. The Government saw these processes as part of a homogeneous civil justice system that integrated IT as a tool to develop community awareness of their legal rights and responsibilities. The objective was that by doing so, the public would be helped to avoid disputes. The Government saw better access to more user-friendly information as "putting a fence at the top of the cliff rather than an ambulance at the bottom"[56]. If a dispute was not preventable, the framework would be there to guide the public whereby they would become able and willing to access a menu of dispute resolution options with litigation being the last resort.

[56] Clause 4.24 Ibid

The vision presented by the Government broke ADR into three streams;

- Alternative Adjudication (By neutrals other than judges)
- Assisted Settlements (Mediation, Conciliation, Early Neutral Evaluation etc.)
- Direct resolution through trade associations etc.

IT was seen as a vital element to allow growth of these ADR approaches. The current law and judicial rulings would be available on the web making it easier to locate legal information and to predict the likely outcome of a case about to enter the court system. Improved understanding would, if the parties were rational, lead to a desire for them to compromise their disputes.

The various ADR techniques would assist them to do this efficiently and without the intervention of the courts. The paper recognised the risks of fragmenting the justice system and constraining the development of the law by parties falling in with precedent that, lacking judicial examination, appeared to fit their situation. However that approach was already present to a degree in that there was an on-line facility identifying precedent in personal injury cases[57] and so it was more likely such application would grow rather than contract or stand still.

One of the programmes for delivery of the Government's strategic vision for the civil justice system was the establishment of a Community Legal Service to provide front line administration and to take responsibility for community education on civil justice matters.

---

[57] www.wire.co.uk

Since their establishment, the Community Legal Service has published a number of public information leaflets that outline legal rights and problem-solving procedures in a number of areas, one of which provided "Alternatives to Court"[58].

2.4.3. The alternatives to court

The leaflet promoted the use of ADR as an option to, or a parallel process with, litigation. They stated the advantages of ADR as:

- Being more flexible;
- Solving a problem faster;
- Being less stressful; and
- Costing less

The leaflet looked in a step by step way at the differences of ADR to litigation, the different outcomes that could be achieved often over and above those available in court e.g. an explanation or an apology. It considered a number of different forms of dispute resolution; mediation and conciliation, arbitration, litigation and the ombudsman amongst others and gave examples of where each might be practical. It also looked at the potential costs and the various service providers.

Each of the foregoing documents; the Discussion Paper, civil. justice.2000 and Alternatives to Court can be seen as a trickle-down stream of data that built towards the Government objectives of modernising the civil justice system in the UK.

Although application may only have been implemented in England and Wales at present, it must surely only be a matter of time before similar structures were put in place in Scotland and Northern Ireland.

---

[58] CLS Leaflet Number 23, 2001

A fundamental part of Government policy is the development of ADR as a realistic option to litigation and as such it is incumbent upon the various strands of the Administration, such as the Scottish Parliament, to look at developing strategies to achieve this national objective.

2.5. The response of the courts in England and Wales

As discussed above, the new Civil Procedure Rules created a platform for parties to attempt to resolve their dispute by ADR (Part 26.4) and gave the Court discretion when awarding costs to take account of the actings of the parties (Part 44).

Following what may be regarded as a bedding-in period for the new rules, the courts have started to take a stronger line with parties who have been unreasonable in not considering ADR. The first warning to them came in November 1999 in the Court of Appeal case, *Dyson & Field v Leeds City Council*[59]. The judgement gave notice that costs could be lost if a party, the defendant in that case, refused unreasonably to try mediation.

In 2000 a judge rejected the application for summary judgement and ordered payment of indemnity costs by the claimant in the case of *Paul Thomas Construction Ltd v Hyland*[60]. The claimant had rejected pre-issue mediation and approaches for negotiation on the issues. The Construction and Engineering Pre-Action Protocol was not yet binding but was widely available in draft form and Judge Wilcox took the view that the terms might have been considered, particularly Clause 5.4. However as it was not binding he said he would not take

---

[59] Unreported 29 November 1999

[60] Paul Thomas Construction Ltd v Hyland & Another, 8/3/00 CILL 6/01 1743

[61] The Times, 8 January 2002

account of it in his judgement but did take account of Section 4 of the Practice Directions Protocol of the Civil Procedure Rules that was applicable at the time.

In the Court of Appeal decision in *Cowl v Plymouth City Council*[61], Lord Woolf refused a judicial review to residents over the closing of a Local Authority home. In his judgement he made a number of remarks that set a course for how the courts would view failure, without good cause, to try ADR;

> *"... insufficient attention is paid to the paramount importance of avoiding litigation whenever this is possible. Particularly in the case of these disputes both sides must by now be acutely conscious of the contribution alternative dispute resolution can make to resolving disputes in a manner which both meets the needs of the parties and saves time, expense and stress."*

In referring to the parties finding themselves locked into the dispute he went on to say;

> *"... the parties should have been able to come to a sensible conclusion as to how to dispose of the issues which divided them. If they could not do this without help, then an independent mediator should have been recruited to assist. That would have been a far cheaper course to adopt."*

In *Dunnett v Railtrack*[62] the appellant lost her claim against Railtrack for compensation for the loss of horses that had got on to the line after work by Railtrack contractors to the parties' boundary fence. Dunnett had lost the initial case and Schiemann LJ had recommended ADR

---

[62] [2002] 2 ALL ER 850

when granting Dunnett leave to appeal. She (Dunnett) approached Railtrack and suggested an ADR procedure. Railtrack refused but did make two separate Part 36 offers to Dunnett. However the Court, in applying the requirements of the Civil Procedure Rules (CPR) Part 44, refused to award Railtrack costs as they had refused to consider mediation before the Appeal.

The judgement in Dunnett addressed a number of important points regarding the English judiciary's position on CPR Parts 26.4 and 44. Railtrack won their case, they made Part 36 offers but the fact that they had refused the offer to mediate was sufficient to prevent them from receiving a costs award.

In his judgement Brooke LJ said;

> "… when asked by the court (Counsel for Railtrack) why his clients were not willing to contemplate ADR, said that this would necessarily involve the payment of money which his clients were not willing to contemplate, over and above what they had already."

The interesting question to be posed here was what money was being referred to?

The only money Railtrack would have expended at that point would have been money in defence of their position. They believed they would be successful in the case and so it proved, they could therefore have been expecting, but for Part 44, to receive their costs.

The cost of a private mediation, of indeterminate duration, would not be recoverable in their situation and yet the court took the view that Railtrack were unreasonable in their stance. This must be regarded as a very powerful message. Another point was that Dunnett was represented by counsel in the Appeal through the Bar's pro bono scheme.

In this case, there was considerable imbalance in the relative resources of the parties and so it may be argued that Railtrack could easily have borne the cost of mediation. Against that they should have been aware that, by refusing to contemplate mediation, they were at risk of being refused their costs.

However, if that argument was valid, then what of the situation where the party being taken to Appeal, in his view wrongly, was the weaker financially and he was faced by the offer to mediate knowing he would have no chance of recovering his costs? Could this be regarded as a bullying tactic by his more powerful adversary who might see it as an opportunity to drain his opponent's resources further at a time when the opponent may face ruin if his costs were not recovered?

The simple answer may be that mediation should have taken place at the outset but if, for whatever reason, it has not, the challenge to the Court would be an interesting one. Could, for example, a complex matter with a long running history be dealt with in a tightly time-controlled mediation to the satisfaction of the parties? Could the mediator be expected to understand detailed documentation any quicker than an adjudicator in a similar situation who was given 28 days as a minimum period to form his view? Costs in the situation would not be inconsiderable. Could an unscrupulous but more financially strong party look to overcomplicate the ADR procedure burdening it with extensive documentation in the knowledge that more time spent mediating would weaken the opposition. This may appear to be a very jaundiced view but the court and the parties would have to be aware of this type of issue when the procedure was, under the CPR, the appropriate forum.

Article 6 of the ECHR was not an issue in the Dunnett case because, in the event of a failed mediation, the case could always have returned to the court but, in situations of unequal financial strength, the dice may in fact be more loaded against the weaker party following Dunnett.

This may be the stick as opposed to the carrot effect of the Government's objective of better case management and fewer cases being litigated when they were better suited to other means of disposal.

Rule 1.1(c) and (d) would be relevant considerations for the court in the Dunnett case as would Rule 1.4(2)(a), (e) and (f). If, however Rules 1.1(e) and 1.4(h) were considered;

"Rule 1.1...allotting to it (the case) an appropriate share of the Court's resources while taking into account to allot resources to other cases."

"Rule 1.4(2):

Active case management includes –

(h) considering whether the likely benefits of taking a particular step justify the cost of taking it;"

Should the court have granted Dunnett leave to appeal in the first place?

A further development of the considerations above, and in whether a refusal to mediate was reasonable, came up in the case of Hurst v Leeming[63].

The case concerned a serial litigant Hurst who had been a partner in a legal firm but had taken failed court action against his former partners. He blamed his counsel Leeming QC for his losses and, after various attempts, took his action against Leeming to court. Following an exchange with the judge, Hurst withdrew has action but claimed he

---

[63] [2001] EWHC Ch 1051

should not be liable for Leeming's costs as he had offered mediation of the dispute to Leeming.

Leeming provided 5 reasons for his refusal to mediate that he believed met the terms of Clause B6 of the Professional Negligence Pre-Action Protocol;

- The legal costs already incurred in meeting the allegations and the threat of proceedings.
- The seriousness of the allegations of professional negligence.
- The total lack of substance of the claims made.
- The lack of any real prospect of success given that Mr Hurst's objective from the mediation was to obtain a financial payment from Mr Leeming when there was no merit in the claim.

The character of Mr Hurst as revealed by his actions – that of a man obsessed with the notion that he was the victim of an injustice and who would not be able or willing to adopt the attitude required if mediation was to have any prospect of success.

Mr Justice Lightman ruled out the first four reasons as not justifying refusal to mediate but held that whether the mediation had any real prospect of success, point 5 of Leeming's argument, was the critical factor. For a range of reasons related to Hurst's dogmatic views, Mr Justice Lightman thought that there was no prospect of a successful mediation in the case and so awarded costs against Hurst.

He emphasised in his judgement that refusal on the grounds stated would be reasonable but that this was a high-risk strategy. He went on to explain;

> *"... for in making this objective assessment of the prospects of mediation, the starting point must surely be the fact that the*

mediation process itself can and does often bring about a more sensible and more conciliatory attitude on the part of the parties than might otherwise be expected to prevail before the mediation, and may produce a recognition of the strengths and weaknesses by each party of his own case and that of his opponent, and a willingness to accept the give and take essential to a successful mediation."

Another issue that has been considered by the courts is the enforcement of contractual agreements to attempt ADR. The case in question was *Cable and Wireless PLC (C&W) v IBM United Kingdom Ltd. (IBM)*[64]. It involved a dispute between C&W and IBM related to the terms of clauses 40 and 41 of a Global Framework Agreement (GFA) under which they would seek to resolve their disputes. Clause 40 was identified as Problem Escalation and Resolution. The clause described an executive tribunal procedure that could be tried at staged levels of seniority within each company failing which;

"If the dispute is not resolved by escalation in accordance with Clause 40.1 the parties shall seek to resolve disputes between them pursuant to Clause 41.2"[65]

Clause 41.2 relates to a reference to ADR.

C&W sought to argue that Clause 41.2 was an agreement to negotiate that had already been found to be unenforceable in *Courtney & Fairbairn Ltd. V Tolaini Brothers (Hotels) Ltd.* [1975] 1 WLR 297. Coleman J rejected that line stating inter alia;

---

[64] [2002] EWHC 2059 (Comm Ct)

[65] Extract from Clause 40 of the GFA

"It is to be observed that the parties have not simply agreed to attempt in good faith to negotiate a settlement. In this case they have gone further than that by identifying a particular procedure, namely an ADR procedure as recommended to the parties by the Centre for Dispute Resolution to which I refer as "CEDR"."

He went on to say;

"The principle of voluntary participation is preserved in Clause 14 of the (CEDR) model procedure[66]: (Coleman J then related Clause 14)....

This provision clearly only provides for withdrawal after the mediator has been appointed and the mediation commenced. It thus envisaged a certain minimum participation in the procedure."

C&W had failed to meet even these minimum criteria and so the judge adjourned the case;

"...until after the parties have referred all their outstanding disputes to ADR."

A case that has produced a different outcome to *Dunnett v Railtrack and Hurst v Leeming is SITA v Watson Wyatt*: Maxwell Batley (Part 20 Defendant)[67].

Maxwell Batley had refused on three occasions to join a mediation between SITA and Watson Wyatt. The reasons they put forward were that the offer to join the mediation had come too late the first time as

---

[66] CEDR Model Mediation Procedure and Agreement 6th Edition
[67] [2002] EWHC Ch 2025

they were unprepared for the process. On the second occasion the judge Park J considered that Watson Wyatt had used inappropriate pressure to bring Maxwell Batley to the table as a means of getting them to contribute to a settlement with SITA. On the third occasion the offer came at a time when Maxwell Batley considered there was inadequate time available before the trial on the matter to also prepare for a mediation. Throughout the period Maxwell Batley took the position that they had a cast-iron case to avoid any liability.

The judgement is controversial on a number of points:

Park J differentiated the case from both Dunnett and Hurst but it is arguable that both cases were pertinent to the outcome. In Dunnett, Railtrack argued unsuccessfully for their costs, having proceeded on the basis that they had a cast-iron case that they did win.

Unlike Hurst, Watson Wyatt were not obsessed with winning and in fact settled with SITA in mediation so one could argue particularly following settlement with SITA a successful mediation in advance of the trial could have avoided significant cost to both parties.

The judge restricted his award of costs to Maxwell Batley to standard basis costs leaving Maxwell Batley to face around £400,000 of further legal costs even though they had been largely successful in their defence.

The judge allowed Maxwell Batley to introduce evidence on disclosures made, specifically by the Mediator from the first mediation. These disclosures, that may be said to have been inappropriate by the Mediator were supportive of Maxwell Batley's line of resisting mediation. The confidentiality of the mediation process was breached with the tacit collusion of the judge.

The court in *Leicester Circuits Ltd v Coates Brothers Plc*[68] provided further support to ADR in that Coates, while being successful in overturning a previous decision in the Appeal Court were refused a significant part of their costs in the lower court, including all the hearing time, because they withdrew from a pre-arranged mediation just prior to it taking place. In the costs judgement of the Appeal Court, Judge LJ said;

> *"It seems to us that the unexplained withdrawal from an agreed mediation process was of significance to the continuation of this litigation…We do not for one moment assume that the mediation process would have succeeded, but certainly there is a prospect that it would have done had it been allowed to proceed."*

The overall conclusion to be drawn from this judgement may be that further training of judges and court officers is necessary to ensure more consistent outcomes in cases where the option to utilise ADR, or failure to do so is being tested.

These judgements, with the exception of SITA, a rogue result, may indicate that the English courts have responded to the Civil Procedure Rules and in that way the Government's objective to encourage parties to go to court as a last resort particularly where there was the opportunity of resolving their disputes by ADR techniques.

2.6. The Scottish perspective

The Scottish judicial procedures and the rules of court have been under examination in recent years principally to develop approaches that improve on or overcome the delays, wasted time and expense that had become endemic in litigation.

---

[68] [2003] EWCA Civ 333

Reforms have been made that do not go as far as Woolf in looking to direct appropriate disputes away from court processes. Instead the objective has been to maintain judicial involvement but streamline its procedures and address the issues that had, in the past, resulted in abortive processes that generated cost and delay for all involved.

The Civil Procedure Rules for Scotland were reformed in 1994 to take account of a report by Lord Coulsfield entitled "Report of the Working Party on Commercial Causes"[69].

The new commercial cause rules "... represent the first conscious attempt in Scotland to implement whole scale case management measures with fully fledged judicial proactivity."[70] The working party had been established as a result of criticism of the arbitration procedures that were seen as being lengthy, expensive and in need of updating[71]. A number of their recommendations were incorporated in the new rules. These included that a full-time court dedicated exclusively to commercial matters was set up. Case management to speed up throughput of cases in this commercial court was a core element of the new rules. Cases were dealt with at three types of hearings; preliminary, procedural and final disposal. There was a system of fixed diets setting a timetable for the procedure that minimised the likelihood of delays and adjournments that were seen as a failing in the previous court arrangements.

The hearings were generally more informal than the previous court procedures. In the preliminary and procedural hearings, the sessions

---

[69] November 1994

[70] The New Commercial Cause Rules, R Clancy Advocate, Scots Law Times News 1997 pp45-49, 53-58

[71] Dispute Resolution and Conflict Management in Construction – An International Review - Fenn, O'Shea and Davies 1998, Scotland p660

took the form of round table meetings where the objective was to design the most effective procedure and timetable to dispose of the dispute. Issues were also narrowed at these "meetings" and some disputes were settled at, or following, the preliminary hearing. The commercial court has one full-time and two part-time judges.

Since implementation of the rules, the court has dealt conclusively with numerous commercial actions. A survey showed that in the four years prior to introduction of the new rules in September 1994 there were on average 50 to 60 commercial cases in court. In the two years following September 1994 there were 286 cases in the commercial court. 87% of these cases were completed within 12 months, with 55% being finished in 6 months.[72]

Following a report by Lord Coulsfield on procedures for personal injury actions, the Rules of the Court of Session were amended to incorporate the recommendations he made. The new rules come into force on 1 April 2003. Rule 43.9(1) concerns pre-trial meetings;

"For the purposes of this rule, a pre-trial meeting is a meeting between the parties, which shall be held not later than four weeks before the date assigned for the proof or trial to discuss –

settlement of the action; and to agree, so far as is possible, the matters which are not in dispute between them."[73]

Lord Coulsfield has written an introduction to the new procedures and in the opening section termed "Background to the Proposals"[74]

---

[72] See 71 ibid

[73] Act of Sederunt (Rules of the Court of Session Amendment No. [X]) (Personal Injury Actions)2002

[74] New Procedures in Personal Injury Actions, Introduction by the Rt Hon Lord Coulsfield

he refers to an earlier report by Lord Cullen[75] following which, a working party was formed "to consider methods of simplifying and streamlining the administration of civil court procedure. The object was to eliminate or reduce undue delay and unnecessary expense for those involved in the litigation process."[76]

He went on to criticise the existing system that resulted in 95% of civil cases settling, with one third settling in the last week before proof. The result was wasted time and expense to all involved including the courts.

Personal Injury cases, that had the even greater settlement rate of 99%, were seen as an area ripe for procedural reform. The whole thrust of the new procedure is to improve efficiency and effectiveness of process. The emphasis is on a timetable, simplified pleadings and a fixed date of proof within 12 months following lodging of defences.

In reference to the pre-trial meeting referred to above, Rule 43.9(1), Lord Coulsfield states its purpose is "... to discuss settlement realistically, or if settlement could not be achieved, to narrow the issues between them.[77]"

The Cullen Report referred to above was examined in the Scots Law Times[78]. Lord Cullen had been asked to review the administration procedures of the Outer House of the Court of Session and to make recommendations for improvement. He made four key recommendations

---

[75] Review of Business of the Outer House of the Court of Session 1995

[76] New Procedures in Personal Injury Actions, Introduction by the Rt Hon Lord Coulsfield

[77] Ibid

[78] The Cullen Report, Nigel Morrison QC Scots Law Times Yearbook 1996 pp 93-100

- Pleadings to be initially in abbreviated form
- Earlier and wider disclosure of evidence.
- Better case management.
- Organisation of business to avoid delays in proofs and jury trials.

The recommendations were aimed at achieving earlier settlements and reducing delay and expense. In production of his report, Lord Cullen considered Woolf and looked at how courts in the USA conducted their business. The report was to focus on procedural improvement to the Outer House and so, possibly for that reason, alternatives outwith the judicial system were not considered. The report concentrated on devising a more effective procedure, achieving a reduction in cost and earlier settlement. One recommendation in case management did hint at ADR when it noted under comments on personal injury claims that following the defender lodging "... a schedule of assessment of the value of the pursuer's claim. The court would then consider whether there should be a debate on the preliminary pleas, explore the manner in which the facts or law can be most suitably resolved (including alternatives to judicial determination [my emphasis])"

The Court of Session has not adopted the recommendations themselves but they have been used as a background for other procedural reform such as the Personal Injury procedures above.

While the Supreme Court of Scotland does not go as far as Lord Woolf's reforms in England and Wales by actually bringing ADR into its case management strategy, there is a clear emphasis on more efficient procedures and the intention for early settlement.

The present route chosen may have two effects:

- If the procedures as reformed continue, as they have started in the Commercial Court, to operate effectively then the impetus will be, as with Personal Injury, to continue to streamline process rather than take the more radical step of formally introducing ADR into the Court System.

- Without the support of judicial reform and the accompanying threat of cost sanctions for unreasonable refusal to try ADR, as included in Woolf, growth in its use will continue to be restricted to more informed parties making it their chosen method.

The Sheriff Court Rules do recognise ADR under Rule 40.12 of the Ordinary Cause Rules with respect to case management;

"40.12(1) At the Case Management Conference in a commercial action the sheriff shall seek to secure the expeditious resolution of the action.

Parties shall be prepared to provide such information as the sheriff may require to determine –....the orders to make to ensure the expeditious resolution of the action.

The orders the sheriff may make in terms of paragraph 2(b) may include but shall not be limited to –....any order which the sheriff thinks will result in the speedy resolution of the action (including the use of alternative dispute resolution), or requiring the attendance of parties in person at any subsequent hearing."[79]

The foregoing clause is the only reference made to ADR in Scottish Court procedures but, despite its introduction in 1993, enquiries to the Sheriff Clerks in Edinburgh and their counterparts in the commercial courts in Glasgow confirmed that they had no recollection of the approach being ordered. The reasons for a failure to adopt an approach that has proved successful south of the Border may be

[79] Courts, Lower: Statutes, Ordinary Cause Rules 1993

explained by the words of Sheriff Nigel Morrison in his article in the Scots Law Times revealing the way ADR is viewed in certain judicial quarters in Scotland;

"We do have to be careful, however, not to price the courts out of the market where the rivals of arbitration, ADR and mediation lurk."[80]

Outwith the courts, statutory forms of ADR have been restricted to arbitration, adjudication, the tribunal system and the ombudsman. Each of these procedural forms has been described earlier and the comments following are restricted to their use in Scotland.

Arbitration has existed in one form or another in Scotland since the thirteenth century[81]. As noted previously it has become at least as slow and expensive as litigation and so has recently been little used for resolution of domestic disputes other than where statutory or contractual requirements specify it[82].

Adjudication as defined in the HGCRA 1996 has become widely used for dispute resolution in the Construction Industry in Scotland and throughout the rest of the UK. Its impact on other forms of ADR will be considered in the next chapter.

Tribunals have been used by the Government as a quick and cost-effective method of resolving disputes related to administrative matters between statutory bodies and the public without the need to resort to the courts. Many types of these tribunals are operated

---

[80] Reform of Civil Procedure SLT Yearbook 1998 p 144

[81] Hunter *The Law of Arbitration in Scotland* (1987)

[82] Footnote 68 supra, Funding ADR in Scotland, Clark and Mays SLT Yearbook 1997 p 29, The ADR Practice Guide, Mackie, Miles, Marsh and Allen Clause 3.5.2, p 54. These are sample comments of what appears to be a general opinion in legal circles.

throughout Scotland including Social Security Appeals Tribunals, Employment Tribunals, National Health Service Tribunals and Immigration Appeals Tribunals. They often sit regionally on a daily basis as public forums and they will deal with many cases in a summary procedure monitored by the Scottish Committee of the Council of Tribunals[83]. Further disputes regarding decisions of the tribunals can be referred to the courts, in specified circumstances, for judicial review or appeals of decisions.

Other forms of ADR would be used as additions to these procedures that would continue to operate in accordance with statute. Many legal practitioners trained as mediators etc. will provide these further on-demand services and two additions to the supply stream in Core Mediation and the Scottish Mediation have been created to respond to the demand for ADR services outwith the statutory framework.

The incentive to develop the use of ADR in the commercial field could come through the pressure created by major indigenous companies in the fields of banking and insurance that operate in the global market. These companies will seek the most effective forms of dispute resolution to suit the business case be it litigation or ADR. Developments internationally to improve access to ADR are also likely to contribute, potentially more significantly, than those that may arise from the response to the changes to the CPR south of the border.

2.6.1. The development of civil dispute resolution in Scotland

It is over two decades since the Scottish Justice Minister indicated a willingness of Government to encourage the use of commercial ADR services when he said:

---

[83] On the authority vested by the Tribunals and Inquiries Act 1958

'The forms of civil dispute resolution should be effective in their working, proportionate to the issues involved and fair in their effects. We should also encourage ways of diverting dispute resolutions away from the courts to mediation and conciliation services where appropriate'.

2.6.1.1. *The report of the Scottish consumer council justice advisory group*

In a report produced by the Scottish Consumer Council in August 2001 called "Consensus Without Court". Scottish Consumer Council (2001) it was noted that:

'While there are a considerable number of trained mediators in Scotland there remains little demand for their services in commercial and consumer disputes'.

Similarly, the Royal Society of Edinburgh in a report produced in January 2002 entitled "Encouraging Resolution – mediating patient/ health services disputes in Scotland" concluded that:

In Scotland ... the use of ADR processes such as mediation is negligible'

That report found that of the approximately 500 medical negligence claims pursued in Scotland each year, 70% were dropped at some stage prior to going to court, 25% were pursued in court but were settled before a hearing and only 5% went to a court hearing. Significantly, however, it was estimated that the time taken to settle a claim from the date when a formal claim was made was on average between three and a half and four and a half years.

A major report into the civil justice system in Scotland produced by The Scottish Consumer Council Justice Advisory Group chaired by Court of Session judge Lord Coulsfield was published in November

2005 entitled "The Civil Justice System in Scotland – a Case for Review? (Scottish Consumer Council, 2005)

The report contained a number of interesting findings. For example, of those who had their dispute decided by a court less than 50% thought the result was fair – interesting as you would always expect to satisfy at least 50% but a result which is probably explained by the costs which even the winner of a court action has to incur.

In contrast 80% of those who had reached a settlement extra-judicially thought they had completely or in part achieved their objective compared to 43% of those who had gone to court.

The report details with the processes available for solving civil justice problems at chapter 5. The report discusses the notion that there should be a "menu of choices" available for parties in dispute ranging from negotiation and mediation at the "least intervention" end of the scale to arbitration and litigation at the "most intervention" end. The report commented that of those choices which might be available a high number of people – 43% - had never heard of mediation.

Nevertheless over 50% of parties actually involved in a dispute said they would have preferred their case to have gone to mediation rather than to court and those surveyed who had gone through mediation were generally "very satisfied" with the process.

2.6.1.2. The response of the Scottish executive

In February 2007 the Scottish Executive issued a report entitled "Modern Laws for a Modern Scotland – A Report on Civil Justice In Scotland[84]".

[84] The background to the decision to undertake a review of the civil courts is set out in Chapter 3 of the report published by the Scottish Government entitled 'Modern Laws for a Modern Scotland' at www.scotland.gov.uk/Resource/Doc/165338/0045028.pdf

The report is in part a response to the Scottish Consumer Council's call for a civil justice review.

It states that

> *"There is a need for an in-depth look at the structure and procedures of the civil courts with a remit to produce recommendations for changes to achieve a system which deals with cases partly within a reasonable time and at a reasonable cost" and appointed Lord Gill to undertake "a comprehensive review of the structure, jurisdiction, procedures and working methods of the civil courts in Scotland".*

The Scottish Executive report suggest that the Scottish government is now very much in favour of mediation becoming part and parcel of the civil justice system in the future following Lord Gill's Review and refers to its support for both the Sheriff Court Rules Council and the Court of Session Rules Council in their consideration of the place of alternative dispute resolution in the court process.

2.6.1.3. The Gill Review of civil justice in Scotland[85]

Lord Gill's Review issued a Consultation Paper in November 2007 which deals with the reform of civil procedure at Chapter 5 and deals specifically with the role of mediation and other methods of dispute resolution at paragraphs 5.16 – 5.28.

It describes the growth of interest in methods of dispute resolution other than formal adjudication by the court as "one of the most notable developments in civil justice over the past decade or so"

---

[85] The Report of the Scottish Civil Courts Review was launched by the Lord Justice Clerk, the Rt Hon Lord Gill, on Wednesday, 30 September 2009. The Report, which is in two volumes, is now available on-line @ http://www.scotcourts.gov.uk/civilcourtsreview/

although it goes on to state that "Scotland has not to date followed the trend evident in some other jurisdictions, where mediation and other methods of dispute resolution are now widely used". It concludes by setting out the eleven areas where the Review will wish to consider evidence about the use of mediation and other methods of dispute resolution to assess whether, and in what circumstances, it can offer an effective complement, supplement or alternative to litigation.

Among the recommendations made within the review of relevance to ADR were those relating to the use of mediation within the Scots court system. The opportunity to introduce procedures for mandatory mediation in appropriate cases or for costs sanction for unreasonable refusal to engage in mediation on the model of the English CPR was not taken. The report also rejected the idea that parties should have to make averments in their pleadings about the steps, if any, they have taken to resolve their dispute by alternative means. Instead the Gill review recommend only some measures to increase public awareness of mediation such as information on the Scottish Court Service website, leaflets and a helpline in addition to the introduction of a mediation service for small claims.

The Gill Review's recommendations led to a number of initiatives including rewriting the rules of civil procedure to make them simpler and less technical (the Rules Rewrite Project) and the creation of the Scottish Civil Justice Council. The Courts Reform (Scotland) Act 2014 also followed the Review and sets out powers to regulate procedure in the Sheriff Court and Sheriff Appeal Court.

Those powers include encouraging the settlement of disputes and the use of ADR. Rule 1.2(4) of the Simple Procedure Rules provides that the

> *'Parties are to be encouraged to settle their disputes by negotiation or alternative dispute resolution, and should be able to do so*

throughout the progress of a case' and Rule 1.8(2) vests the sheriff with powers to 'do anything or give any order considered necessary to encourage negotiation or alternative dispute resolution between the parties.'

Both provisions aim to enhance the role of ADR within the court process and require the parties and the courts to adopt a more active and constructive approach to settlement and the ADR procedures in helping to achieve the settlement of disputes

2.6.1.4. The Scottish parliament's justice committee review on ADR in civil justice

In 2019, a tide of analysis of evidence and proposals for change has come together. Review by the Justice Committee of the Scottish Parliament was followed by consultation on a draft private member's Mediation Bill. The Scottish Government's modernisation agenda has included commissioning, in 2017 and 2018, independent reviews of publicly aided funding for legal services, and separately the regulation of legal services. Funding for legal services was subject to independent review from 2017 onwards. Rethinking Legal Aid: An Independent Strategic Review in February 2018 promoted the idea of wider support for a range of dispute resolution for disputants, not all in the hands of lawyers (Evans, 2018).

An International Evidence Review (APS Group Scotland, 2019), was commissioned by the Scottish Government, and an Expert Group established by Scottish Mediation reported (Scottish Mediation, 2019) and was acknowledged by the Scottish Government (Ross, 2021). Collectively, these air the prospect of parties being steered towards mediation as a form of court annexed dispute resolution in the early stages of civil cases by provision of early information on mediation, and presumptive steer towards mediation in civil cases (with some excepted categories). The Scottish Government's National Performance Framework and annual published justice priorities point towards choice, empowerment and resilience for individuals and communities.

The Scottish Government has extolled access to a range of dispute resolution options for decades, but without putting sustained public funding behind them. Responding to the 2009 Report of the Scottish Civil Courts Review (the Gill Report), the Scottish Government sought to 'modernise civil and criminal law and the justice system to meet the needs of people in Scotland in the 21st century'.

A specific work package was dedicated to Dispute Resolution for which the Scottish Legal Aid Board was the lead agency, until the establishment of a Scottish Civil Justice Council by legislation in 2013.

The independent *Fit for the Future: Report of the Independent Review of Legal Services Regulation* aired support for lawyers to work alongside mediators and others in multi-option firms and notes that early resolution options for complaints about legal services should exist akin to mediation that had been offered successfully by the Scottish Legal Complaints Commission (Robertson, 2018). Some of the recommendations made in these independent reports have met resistance from the legal profession and were being deliberated upon by the Scottish Government prior to absorption of government time on coronavirus issues. The concerns of the legal profession about the impact of coronavirus on business and financial sustainability of lawyers is unlikely to increase, from its low level, their appetite for sharing the legal services market.

During its work on ADR, the Scottish Parliament's Justice Committee requested further information from the Lord President's Private Office on current training provided to the judiciary in relation to ADR. The reply suggests that some training is provided by the Judicial Institute, although this varies from year-to-year and is usually as part of a broader course.

The simple procedure training courses in 2016 and 2017 highlighted the obligation on courts to consider ADR. A Simple Procedure Toolkit is also available to the judiciary, which includes guidance on the appropriateness and availability of mediation. The Scottish courts have a central role to play in ensuring the effective and early resolution of disputes. However, existing court rules take different approaches towards alternative dispute resolution.

Moreover, some sheriffs and judges appear to be more willing to encourage or refer parties to ADR than others. While accepting that there needs to be some flexibility on a case-by-case basis, there also needs to be more consistency shown by the judiciary in relation to the use of ADR.

Although the recommendations by the Justice Committee are wide ranging, some of the key proposals of the Report include the introduction of a degree of compulsion to encourage the parties to consider mediation and the introduction of primary legislation in the form of a Mediation Act. The proposed law seeks to take the bold step to put mediation on a legislative footing.

2.7. Summary

The Civil Procedure Reforms that followed the report by Lord Woolf responded to the various issues affecting the existing process of dispute disposal.

The first being growing criticism of the escalating legal costs of commercial disputes and the protracted time involved in a procedure that could be prolonged to the point where the initial cause of the dispute was often reduced in significance relative to the legal costs involved in its resolution.

Secondly the changes in how other jurisdictions were addressing their disputes where potential trade partners in the USA, the Commonwealth, Europe and Asia would be more focused on efficient and economic dispute disposal avoiding the legal process.

Thirdly the effect of the escalating costs of dispute resolution in the UK was that only those supported by Legal Aid or substantial resources were capable of running a dispute to its conclusion denying the bulk of the population access to justice.

Finally, the growth in the Legal Aid bill for the Government was unsustainable in the long term. These issues and how the new CPR addressed them have been considered in this chapter.

There is no doubt that ADR needs judicial development in Scotland, but the examples of England and Wales would be increasingly hard to ignore if the courts were to achieve the same level of "access to justice" for the public.

Similar reforms to the civil Legal Aid system as those made in England and Wales may be the catalyst necessary to expand the use of the consensual forms of ADR as the preferred method of dispute resolution.

Although as noted above there was a resistance to this level of change in Scotland. International pressure for change both through business and the European Union combined with an expanding knowledge base on ADR may be a more effective contributor to growth.

References

Ancillary Relief Pilot Scheme (Family Courts) (1996) Rules 2.71 to 2.77 of the Family Proceedings Rules 1991 contain the procedure for the Pilot Scheme.

Chornenki, G., (1997). Mediating commercial disputes: Exchanging "power over" for "power with". *Rethinking Disputes: The Mediation Alternative*, 159.

CEDR (2001) Code of Conduct for mediators and other third-party neutrals. CEDR

CEDR (2001) Model Contract Clauses - Fast track drafting guide to key dispute resolution clauses,

CEDR (2001) Model Mediation Procedure & Agreement 8th Edition October 2002

CEDR (2001) Model Early Neutral Evaluation Agreement including guidance notes,

CEDR (2001) Model Expert Determination Agreement including guidance notes,

CEDR (2001) Model Executive Tribunal Procedure including guidance notes, CEDR

CEDR (2001) Model Settlement Agreement & Tomlin Order, CEDR 2001

CEDR (2001) Model ADR Contract Clauses – How and why, Model Contract Clauses, CEDR.

Civil.Justice (1998) Resolving and Avoiding Disputes in the Information Age. A Lord Chancellor's Department Consultation Paper. September. "www.dca.gov.uk/consult/itstrat/civindex.htm". October 14, 2005 (civil justice: Resolving and Avoiding Disputes in the Information Age 1998).

Civil.Justice (2000) A Vision – A Vision of the Civil Justice System in the Information Age. A Lord Chancellor's Department Strategy Paper. June. "www.dca.gov.uk/cj2000/cj2000fr.htm". October 14, 2005 (civil. justice. 2000 – A Vision of the Civil Justice System in the Information Age 2000).

Fenn, P. ed., (1998). *Dispute resolution and conflict management in construction: An international review*. Taylor & Francis.

Genn, H., 1998. The central London county court pilot mediation scheme. *Evaluation report*.

Lord Chancellor's Department (1999) Alternative Dispute Resolution – A Discussion Paper by the Lord Chancellor's Department including responses to survey data. – November.

Macfarlane, J., (1997). *Rethinking disputes: the mediation alternative*. E. Montgomery Publications.

Mackay, A.D., (1989). The Law of Arbitration in Scotland by RLC Hunter.

Menkel-Meadow, C.A.R.R.I.E., (1996). Will Managed Care Give Us Access to Justice? *Achieving Civil Justice: Appropriate Dispute Resolution for the 1990s. R. Smith, (ed.)*. London, Legal Action Group, pp.94-117.

Robertson, D. and Young, G., (2018). An Evaluation of Rent Regulation Measures within Scotland's Private Rented Sector.

Woolf, H., (1995). *Access to Justice: Interim report to the Lord Chancellor on the civil justice system in England and Wales* (Vol. 1). Lord Chancellor's Department.

Case Law

Cable and Wireless PLC (C&W) v IBM United Kingdom Ltd. (IBM) 2002] EWHC 2059 (Comm Ct)

Courtney & Fairbairn Ltd. V Tolaini Brothers (Hotels) Ltd. [1975] 1 WLR 297

Dunnett v Railtrack[2002] 2 ALL ER 850

Hurst v Leeming [2001] EWHC Ch 1051

Leicester Circuits Ltd v Coates Brothers Plc [2003] EWCA Civ 333

Paul Thomas Construction Ltd v Hyland & Another, 8/3/00 CILL 6/01 1743

Chapter Three: Evolution of Dispute Resolution in the Construction Industry

3.1 Introduction

> *It's unwise to pay too much, but it is worse to pay too little. When you pay too much, you lose a little money - that is all. When you pay too little you sometimes lose everything, because the thing you bought was incapable of doing the thing it was bought to do. The common law of business balance prohibits paying a little and getting a lot - it can't be done. If you deal with the lowest bidder, it is well to add something for the risk you run and if you do that you will have enough to pay for something better!! John Ruskin (1819-1900) (Riches & Dancaster, 2004)*

The sentiment expressed by Ruskin could apply to many of the paymasters in today's construction industry. This chapter describes the nature and characteristics of construction disputes, their causes and their effects with particular reference to the UK construction sector.

3.2. Nature of the construction industry

The most consistent shortcoming of the construction industry has been its optimism that the impossible can be surmounted – and in reality, it is often the case. This optimism encourages high-risk strategies in construction projects which can lead to disputes (Riches & Dancaster, 2004). In fairness to the industry, construction projects are very often novel involving clients, designers, contractors and subcontractors who have not previously worked together. The largely unregulated industry also can have difficulty coming to terms with (Campbell, 1997):

- reduced workload and therefore more competitive tendering;
- technological revolution requiring more highly skilled personnel;
- reduced 'on-the-job' training;
- increased legislation, particularly in health and safety;
- new methods of procurement;
- many ad-hoc forms of contract; and
- an increasingly litigious climate.

Many commentators believe that adversarial attitudes have intensified over recent years. This is hardly surprising given the competitive nature of the industry, in which contractors tender unrealistically low prices and schedules to obtain contracts, predictably leading to project cost and time overruns.

Many believe that it is common for contractors to bid for projects with their claim potential in mind as a means of improving their profit margin. Such tactics provide a fertile breeding ground for disputes to develop and despite contracting parties' best efforts to avoid them, they all too often occur.

3.3. The construction industry's problems

The construction industry and its products are vast. The industry touches all of our lives every day. The roads we drive to work on, the places we live and work, where our children are educated, where we seek our health care and where we shop. These are all products of the collective that forms the construction industry.

Some time has passed since Ruskin's statement was made and the construction industry has moved on at a great pace. Both its structure and products have changed markedly over this period, embracing new techniques and materials. However, the big question is whether the 'culture' has changed. The industry, although some would argue it is all too easy to enter, continues to remain a market of high risk. In the period which followed the Second World War, the industry was dependent on government work which created the boom or bust syndrome. The latter-day economics of the free market has been no kinder to the fortunes of the industry. Every building and civil engineering contract is a prototype. It is produced, not in the warm and dry and consistent climate of the factory but in the field, its permanent home.

A building is built on many relationships. There are contracts between contractors, suppliers, subcontractors, sub-sub-contractors and those professional relationships of design and administration. The construction society has evolved to be more competitive and more litigious. The role of the professions has become devalued by the excesses of competition and where once it was unthinkable to question the word of a professional, the professional negligence suit has become more frequent. There are specialists in construction litigation and arbitration and a separate industry of claims consultants has grown to meet the demand for resolution of the industry's combative approach to disputes.

There are many specialist legal publications and law reports devoted to construction but the construction dispute is not a new and radical concept. Disputes have always been an inevitable part of the construction industry. The number of relationships alone required to produce a structure of any magnitude militates toward this inevitability. There is a significant amount of case law on construction disputes with an overwhelming number of these related to arguments over the recovery of costs.

These types of disputes typically attract significant media and public attention, which is likely to put further strain on relationships between the disputing parties and cast a shadow over their reputations in the construction industry. We know the main reasons why disputes occur in the construction industry in the UK which would suggest that steps can be taken and measures put in place to reduce the number and reform how construction projects are run. If and when disputes do arise, there are numerous alternative methods for resolution which can be implemented to amicably and relatively quickly reach a mutually acceptable conclusion but the number of disputes remains high.

Although most construction claims are settled by negotiation, many become disputes requiring resolution. Such disputes have been described as 'prolongation and aggression', which feed on each other making dispute resolution in the industry 'conspicuously exhausting of time, energy, money and spirit'. Traditionally, such resolution would have been by either arbitration or litigation. However, disillusionment with these processes and a growing need to change has long been recognised by many in the construction industry and the legal profession.

3.4. Construction contracts: A predictable source of conflict

Many who are involved in the construction industry believe that conflict is inevitable and that this is promoted by the standard forms of contract used. However, the potential for conflict is inherent in any contractual situation. All parties involved have the same objective, that is sharing in the profit or benefit from the project.

Profit for a contractor and for the promoter of the building is earned in different ways.

It is often assumed that when the profit position of either party is threatened, conflict will emerge. The potential for conflicts, disputes and claims will always exist and it is beneficial to recognise this from the beginning of any contractual relationship. It is also worth considering the distinction between these terms to provide a basis for understanding.

A claim is no more than an assertion and cannot become a dispute until there is a genuinely disputable issue. The dispute resolution process in the contract cannot necessarily determine conflict. A dispute arises if there is a genuine difference of opinion regarding the interpretation and implementation of the contract. While any difference of view is respected by the parties, no conflict yet exists – simply a dispute. Naturally, conflict can follow and this depends on the behaviour of those involved in the dispute.

3.5. The provision for ADR in construction contracts

In the UK, the most common form of standard for construction contracts is the Joint Contracts Tribunal (JCT) contract and, since the early 21st century, the New Engineering Contract (NEC). Internationally, one of the most widely used standard form contracts is from the Federation Internationale des Ingenieurs-Counseils (International Federation of Consulting Engineers - FIDIC). These standard forms of contract all contain specific ADR provisions.

3.5.1. The JCT contract

The JCT Design and Build Contract was redrafted in 2005 to comply with the HGCRA 1996. Although a new suite of JCT contracts was published in 2016, this latest set of contract documents feature the same ADR provisions as the 2005 JCT.

The JCT contract provides for the resolution of disputes via a range of ADR methods. Clause 9.1 refers to mediation and ADR and confirms that the JCT supports the use of these forms of ADR when appropriate.

It is suggested that the institution or body and method used to resolve the dispute should be determined according to the characteristics of the dispute (Hughes et al, 2015). This recognises that the method of ADR to be used to resolve any particular construction dispute depends on the nature and subject matter. The potentially high costs involved in litigation should operate as an incentive for parties to opt-in (JCT, Clause 9.1). Clause 9.2 refers to adjudication, which creates a contractual right for the parties to refer a dispute to this form of ADR, while Clause 9.3 provides the option to refer a dispute to arbitration. Finally, Clause 9.7 provides the basis for litigation and states that it is to be subject to the jurisdiction of the English courts unless the parties have amended the contract to select a different jurisdiction. The JCT is designed for and applies in the law and practice of England and Wales which suggests that it is not appropriate for international construction projects (Safina, 2014). It is argued that a standard form contract that seeks to apply internationally must be suitable for more than a single country (Purba & Prastowo, 2020). Important issues such as liquidation damages caps, rigorous design warranties and currency exchange risk are not addressed in the JCT standard form contract, perhaps because the FIDIC is a more widely used standard form contract, particularly for international construction contracts.

3.5.2. The FIDIC contract

FIDIC was formed in 1913 by the national associations of consulting engineers of Switzerland, France and Belgium and has grown to represent more than 80 countries.

It has established standard form contracts that are used for civil engineering in the majority of countries, particularly those in the developing world (Seppala, 1991). FIDIC published its first international standard form contract in 1957 and has since created several other types of contracts. An entirely new suite of contracts was created in 1999. The new suite includes the Red Book 1999, the Yellow Book 1999, the Silver Book 1999, the Gold Book 2008 and the White Book 2006. The 2017 version of the FIDIC Red Book sought to update the 1999 version by facilitating a more appropriate balancing of risk and reducing the potential for disputes, thereby increasing the likelihood that projects would be completed successfully and on time (Brink, 2021). The publication of the updated Red Book was a strategic step given that it is one of the most widely used standard forms of contracts in international construction (Al-Hyari, 2020). The dispute resolution provisions were significantly amended in the 2017 Red Book pursuant to the broader goal of FIDIC to promote overall avoidance of disputes (Lumbwe, 2020).

The DAB was also assigned a new role in dispute avoidance, and its title changed to Dispute Avoidance and Adjudication Board (DAAB). This change means that the DAAB can now provide non-binding advice and informal assistance to the parties, upon request (Cotovelea, 2021). There are several key features of the new dispute resolution provisions under the new 2017 Red Book. For example, it created a distinction between dispute resolution and claims by placing them into two separate clauses (Mahnken, 2018). This is based on the objective of emphasising that a dispute does not automatically arise simply because a claim has been submitted. Additionally, the role played by the engineer during the administration of the contract has changed, in that they are now under an obligation to encourage the parties to reach an agreement regarding a claim and to act neutrally when making a claim determination (Brink, 2021).

The new Red Book has also added the principle of advance warning, which seeks to encourage the parties to collaborate to resolve potential problems before they develop into actual disputes. Overall, the new version emphasises the need for reciprocity between parties' obligations and the endeavour to avoid disputes from arising.

The 2017 FIDIC Red Book splits dispute resolution into two clauses, which has the effect of creating a distinction between the dispute and claims procedures. Clause 20 deals with the claims of both parties, while Clause 21 applies to dispute resolution. This encourages the parties to avoid disputes and to prevent them from arising purely because a claim has been made. This is further facilitated by the Red Book's specifically distinct definitions of claims and disputes.

A claim is defined as 'a request or assertion by one party to the other party for an entitlement or relief [...] in connection with, or arising out of, the contract or the execution of the works' (Clause 1.1.16).In contrast, a dispute is defined as '(a) any situation where one party makes a claim against the other party [...] (b) the other party [...] rejects the claim in whole or in part and (c) the first party does not acquiesce' (Clause 1.1.29). Clause 20 applies to the claims of both contractors and employers, applying the same procedure to both. This represents the adoption of a neutral approach toward contracting parties. The Clause uses the term 'the claiming party', which is party-neutral and places emphasis on neutrality. If a claim is made, the claiming party must submit a detailed claim within 84 days. However, if the claim has continuing effect, the submission of the fully detailed claim is deemed to be interim, meaning that it must be followed by monthly submissions. The final submission must be made not more than 28 days after the continuing effect ceases to have an effect. Once a fully detailed claim is received, the engineer must conduct an assessment by consulting with both parties. They must encourage the parties to reach an agreement that is binding within 42 days and failure to reach such an agreement may be deemed to have been rejected (Clause 20). This will then result in the referral of the dispute to the DAAB, which is also the case if a Notice of Dissatisfaction is submitted by either party.

The FIDIC Golden Principles (2019: Principle 5) state that 'unless there is a conflict with the governing law of the contract, all formal disputes must be referred to a [DAAB] for a provisionally binding decision as a condition precedent to arbitration'. The DAAB is an extremely important mechanism because it enables the parties to resolve a dispute more quickly and more cheaply than if it were to be sent to arbitration (Cotovelea, 2021). The DAAB is an independent, neutral panel that decides on a dispute. The decision may take the form of advice or an opinion, if requested by either of the parties, regarding any matter related to the contract.

Alternatively, it may make an award if an official dispute is submitted by either of the parties (Hinchey, 2020). To achieve this, the DAAB must make periodic visits to the site and remain updated with all activities, problems and progress at the site and encourage the avoidance of disputes and the amicable resolution of any that arise (Eble & Furner, 2018).

Finally, the DAAB must conduct an official dispute resolution procedure professionally, which includes the review of the evidence, hearings and issuing a final decision. The DAAB's existence in construction projects has the benefit of facilitating mutual agreement between the parties if an issue arises which could potentially lead to a dispute. Experience demonstrates that the DAAB promotes cooperation and trust, positive relationships and open communication between the parties (Gerber, 2013).

The main reason underlying this is that the DAAB handles disputes individually, which reduces the development of unresolved claims and avoids the development of conflict.

There are both advantages and disadvantages of the DAAB. Key advantages are that DAAB members, due to their presence at the project site, become a part of the team. This means that they can become more adept at identifying problems during the various stages of the project. They also typically have a high level of construction expertise and experience which ensures that any decision made by the DAAB is more accurate (Van Langelaar, 2015).

Periodic site visits enable DAAB members to remain familiar with the progress of the project and to anticipate any problems or potential disputes. The existence of the DAAB also has a positive effect in terms of preventing claims from developing into disputes (Mahken, 2018). By dealing with each claim in an individual manner, the DAAB prevents their accumulation.

A further advantage relates to time. The DAAB must provide its decision within 84 days and so decisions are made relatively quickly, which directly responds to the time-sensitive nature of construction disputes. In comparison to other methods of dispute resolution, the DAAB is cheaper (Chapman, 2009) and the DAAB is independent and impartial, meaning that the parties will be more likely to accept its decisions. Overall, the DAAB provides a means of insurance for parties, enabling them to potentially resolve any dispute that could arise and to prevent disputes from arising in the first place.

In comparison to its advantages, there are few disadvantages. The DAAB adds to the cost of the project, but this is offset by the savings made on disputes (Owen & Totterhill, 2008). Additionally, although the decision of the DAAB is binding on the parties (unless a Notice of Dissatisfaction is made), its enforcement is less authoritative than court judgements or arbitral awards. Overall, the advantages of the DAAB greatly outweigh the disadvantages, meaning that it is a key mechanism in the resolution and prevention of construction disputes.

3.6. Existence of disputes

A dispute can be defined as a situation where a claim has been rejected, in part or in whole, or has simply been ignored by the other party (*Fastrack Contractors Ltd v Morrison Construction Ltd* [2000] BLR 168). In practice, whether or not a dispute exists may not always be so clear-cut. One party may avoid rejecting the claim and, as often occurs in construction, may request further information about it.

If the claimant commences adjudication or arbitration proceedings, the responding party then argues that the condition precedent for such processes – a dispute – has not yet arisen, resulting in a dispute about a dispute. However, according to Saville J:

> *'[b]ecause one man can be said to be indisputably wrong does not, in my view entail that there was therefore never any dispute between them' (Hayter v Nelson Home Insurance [1990] 2 LR 265)*

The courts have also held that if parties cannot agree, then the claimant is entitled to arbitration (*Ellerine Brothers v Klinger* [1982] 1 WLR 1375). Whether or not a dispute exists is significant if the dispute resolution clause requires any dispute to be referred to arbitration and one of the parties seeks resolution through the court[86]. Where a dispute does exist, the court will be required to grant a stay of litigation (sist in Scotland) pending arbitration unless the arbitration agreement is 'null and void, inoperative or incapable of being performed'[87].

3.7. Disputes

It has been widely recognised that 'so long as human nature is what it is there will always be disputes. And those disputes, whatever their

[86] Halki Shipping Corporation v Sopex Oils Ltd (1997) CILL where the Court of Appeal held, by a majority of two to one, that a stay of litigation should be allowed even when it appeared that the defendant had no grounds in support of its refusal to pay. They relied on Hayter v Nelson and so the word 'dispute' was given its widest ordinary meaning.

[87] Arbitration Act 1996, s9 (4)

character, must be resolved – if society is to exist in a civilised way – as quickly, as cheaply and as satisfactorily as possible'(Hellard, 1988). In any construction project, there are several parties involved including the project manager, employer, engineer, sub-contractor and contractor.

Each will have a distinct agreement and there will inevitably be a different understanding of the project and contract requirements. This may result in claims and, ultimately, disputes. There is always a risk of conflict as this is an inherent part of human nature, particularly in the construction industry where the parties compete with each other to maximise their profits. The construction industry has its own 'built-in recipe for conflict', in that the term 'contracting' itself expressly states the nature of the works being carried out (Mackie et al, 2000).

Construction disputes arise when a difference of opinion emerges between two or more persons who interact with each other in some way or another. DeBono (1990) identifies four key categories of disputes, which are known as the 'four F's':

- Fear: The fear of losing one's project or job, or of disapproval of one's skill level or work rate.
- Force: The commencement and end of the use of emotional or physical force. However, in organizations, and the majority of society, morale has a significant impact.
- Fair: The notion that something 'is not fair' can have a highly motivational effect.
- Funds: To participate in a conflict, one must have the financial means. This is a particularly important aspect of constriction disputes, partly due to the long and expensive nature of dispute resolution. Tactically, this can be delayed or extended by the parties to see whether one will fun out of funds quicker.

The 'four F's' are used by organisations as a basis for managing their environment and mitigating potential disputes. DeBono's work plays a major role in explaining why disagreements arise (DeBono, 1990). He suggests various reasons for why individuals interpret things differently and offers an explanation for such reasons to reduce tensions.

While it is beyond the scope of this study to consider each reason in turn, it is apt to consider some of the most pertinent. For example, mood plays a key role in affecting and forming a person's judgement. If an individual has a reputation for being argumentative, they may be more likely to entertain a dispute than a person who is less argumentative and more relaxed and who will be more likely to seek to resolve the issue. A further element is the situation under the dispute resolution process. If it is known that the party is involved in something that has the potential to affect dispute negotiations, it may be more appropriate to avoid entering into the dispute resolution process. A further issue which is often at the heart of commercial disputes is its limited view. This relates to the point at which the parties are committed to their own 'ways' – they may have similar aims for resolving the dispute, but they will be likely to seek outcomes that are entirely different. Finally, a difference in information is also important. By their very nature, disputes arise because the parties have a different understanding of a single problem (Kaufmann and Stern,1988).

This is extremely common in the construction industry given that communication is a management mechanism that has yet to reach its full potential. Many projects intend to use a sophisticated system for managing communication and ensuring that all parties are sufficiently informed. However, where a single member expresses resistance, this has the potential to jeopardise the whole project. Such elements provide the foundations for enabling parties to understand disputes, which can assist them in both avoiding and managing disputes.

3.8. Disputes in the construction industry

The construction industry is quite distinct from other industries in that each construction project is unique. Construction projects can be extremely complex and are typically subject to challenging deadlines without comprising on quality.

During difficult financial periods, it is not uncommon for a contractor to submit a tender at a low price to be awarded a project and to remain in business.

This has been confirmed by studies which show that construction project prices decline significantly during recessions (Cannon et al, 2016). For example, when the global financial crisis began in 2007, the cost of construction contracts greatly decreased with the exception of infrastructure, which marginally increased, as is typically the case during recession periods (Department for Business Innovation & Skills, 2013). This is then typically followed by disputes and claims relating to delays and requests for additional works by the employer. Whatever the basis of a dispute may be, it is almost certain that some type of dispute will arise in a construction contract.

El-Sayegh et al. (2020) identified 27 sources of disputes and divided them into five groups: designer, owner, contractor, contractual and other.

Table 3.1. *Sources of Construction Disputes (after El-Sayegh et al.,2020)*

	Sources of disputes
Designer-related	Time limitation in the design phase
	Poor design
	Inadequate or incomplete technical plans/specification
	Poor preparation and approval of drawings
	Material change and approval during the construction phase
Owner-related	Slowness of the owner's decision-making process
	Inadequate early planning of the project
	Failure to make interim awards on extensions of time and compensating by the owner
	Variations initiated by the owner (additive/deductive)
	Poor Financing by the owner
Contractor-related	Low financing by the contractor during construction
	Shortage and unproductive workers
	Inadequate site investigation
	Poorly defined scope of work
	Poor supervision and site management
	Unsuitable leadership style of construction/project manager
	Underestimation and incompetence of contractors
Contractual	Poorly written contracts
	Differing site conditions
	Contract amendments
	Contradictory and inaccurate information in the contract documents
Other	Obtaining permit/approval from the municipality/ different government authority
	Modifying legislation and regulations
	Inappropriate weather conditions
	Impact on locality in terms of noise, traffic and pollution/ contamination
	Lack of communication and coordination between parties during construction
	Impact of local cultures and social values in the settlement of conflicts

This is illustrative of much of the literature which takes a very pragmatic approach to dispute identification. McGeorge et al (2008) argue that much of the construction dispute resolution literature seems to be highly arbitrary, highly selective and lacking any theoretical grounding.

They further note that many of the researchers used the terms claim and dispute interchangeably at times and at others differentiate. The studies were diverse in their methodological approach in attempting to uncover the sources of disputes ranging from simplistic perception surveys of the industry to analysis of quantifiable project data on disputes and consideration of published legal cases.

3.8.1. Construction disputes – Nature or nurture?

It has been said that the adversarial nature of the construction industry has created a hostile and litigious environment (Bishop et al, 2009) where disputes are common place. There are many studies that back up this assertion however, there is also a growing number of studies that promote more positive business relationships, highlighting an acceptance that there is a need for change within the industry. Over the last few years, Arcadis have undertaken an annual study of the types of disputes arising out of construction contracts to establish an understanding of the construction industry both geographically and globally. In their Global Construction Disputes Report 2020 they conclude that, in 2019, the 5 most common causes of construction disputes in the UK were:

- A failure to properly administer the contract
- Employer, contractor or subcontractor failing to understand and/ or comply with its contractual obligations
- Poorly drafted or incomplete and unsubstantiated claims
- Conflicting party interests (subcontractor / main contractor / employer or Joint Venture partner)

- Incomplete design information or Employer Requirements (for Design and Build)

This is in comparison to the global market where the top 5 most common construction disputes were recorded as being:

- Failure to administer the contract
- Poorly drafted or incomplete and unsubstantiated claims
- Errors and/or omissions in the Contract document
- Failure to understand and comply with its contractual obligations by the Employer / Contractor / Subcontractor
- Failure to make interim awards on Extension of Time and Completion

When comparing the UK industry with the global market, it is apparent that some of the main dispute areas encountered in the UK are generic across the world. Interestingly, the Arcadis report notes that, globally, where a joint venture was in place almost one third of the disputes encountered were driven by a joint venture related difference. In order to establish if the implementation of collaborative business relationships can have a positive impact in preventing construction disputes, it is beneficial to have an understanding of why construction dispute arise, whether the nature of the industry means that disputes are always going to be there requiring input from third parties to resolve or whether differences of opinion crystallise into a dispute because that's historically the mind-set that develops in those working in the industry, passed down through the generations.

3.8.1.1. The nature argument

Akintan and Morledge (2013) brought together research to conclude that traditional procurement is the dominant procurement form in the

UK construction industry and has been since the industrial revolution in the nineteenth century. The RICS draft guidance note[88] advises that the traditional approach is perhaps still popular with those in the construction industry because it is something that they are familiar with as opposed to because it is fit for purpose, listing some advantages and disadvantages of its use. There is no shortage of case law covering all manner of disputes in relation to construction projects. That, coupled with the numerous research papers that refer to the construction industry as "fragmented", give the impression that it is the nature of the industry that leads many contracts down the dispute route.

In a study by Kale and Arditi (2001) it is suggested that it is the quality of the relationship between the contractor and the subcontractor that affects the contractor's ability to perform on projects. Atkintan and Morledge (2013) suggest that the current construction industry is so specialised that there is no one organisation that can provide all of the specialisms required therefore there is a dependence by the main contractor on the smaller, specialist subcontractors to deliver their contracted works.

By taking these two facts together it can be concluded that it is essential for these two parties to form a strong working relationship for the project to be measured as a success. A similar view is taken by Batt and Purchase (2004). They suggest that performance is dependent on activities and performance of others and therefore the quality of the relationship impacts on this.

Black et al (1999) report that there are 4 main perceived failings of traditional adversarial relationships: exploitation is common; specifications are rigid decisions are made with limited knowledge and;

---

[88] RICS Draft Guidance Note – Comparative construction and engineering contracts, https://consultations.rics.org/consult.ti/comparative.construction/view?objectId=2425044

there is a focus on the short term. Part of the logic behind collaborative relationships is that there is a focus on building lasting relationships that are driven by the promise of a future workload. However, Cox and Thompson (1997) draw comparison to the collaborative models in the manufacturing industry and note their limited use in construction based on their opinion that, in the construction industry, repetition is rare and works are typically procured on a one-off basis. They also consider the fact that traditionally, relationships in the construction industry have been conducted from afar, where contracts are often awarded through competitive tender, procuring the lowest priced supplier, leading to adversarial relations and opportunistic behaviour. The construction industry is primarily driven by time and cost. All projects have a timeframe in which they are to be built and a budget that is determined often long before the project commences. Quite often it is the case that this focus on time and cost that can lead to disputes arising.

3.8.1.2. The nurture argument

The other argument is that it is not the nature of the industry that leads to disputes but more so the attitudes and expectations of those involved in the industry that lead to such a high number of disputes arising in the industry. It is possible that, as it is evident that there is a long history of disputes in the construction industry, the crystallising and defending of the dispute is passed down through the generations that often success is measured on one's ability to "win" in a claim situation. Barlow et al (1997) conclude that that partnering is not purely the implementation of a set of practices or techniques but its success is reliant on attitudes being changed along with behaviours. One of the key factors in preventing construction disputes is trust. Briscoe et al (2001) highlight that, in order for there to be significant improvements in the construction supply chain operation, there is a need for investment in new skills with an emphasis being placed on open relationships to reduce the distrust that is common within the industry. Interviews were undertaken during this study and the analysis of these interviews revealed that there were significant attitudinal barriers between the subcontractors and the main contractors. These barriers included a perception that main contractors took advantage of the weaker subcontractors and that these were unlikely to improve as "the leopard could not change its spots".

Humphries et al (2003) draw on other research to conclude that, in the context of construction, working behaviour is often negatively affected by the fact that main contractors realised that by driving down the price of their subcontractors they are increasing their potential cost savings therefore it is common place for unfair practices to prevail with most relationships still being dominated by the perceived power of the participants.

With this in mind, the atmosphere of suspicion that is founded on previous behaviour, has resulted in many companies being reluctant to work to build closer relationships with their adversaries (Moore et al, 1992). Another essential factor which can impact on the presence of disputes in the construction industry is co-operation. It is all very well when a company is vociferous in its support of working with the other players in a project and this process has support from senior management however, if there is a lack of willingness to co-operate at interpersonal or operational levels within the organisation then the entire process can be undermined (Bresnen and Marshall, 2002). Communication is also a key contributor to the crystallising of disputes. It is commonly understood that contractors are used to being secretive with their information.

3.8.1.3. The case law story

Where consultants are employed there is scope for disputes to arise. An example of this is in the case of *Costain v Charles Haswell* (Wood and Ellis, 2005) whereby a claim was brought against Haswell in relation to damages for breach of contract and/or negligence, with Costain alleging that Haswell had produced a design that was defective and that they had incurred significant additional cost and delay to the works as a result. Although Costain came out of the case victorious, they were subject to criticism over an over-inflated claim and their conduct during the proceedings and both parties being criticised over their attitude to settling the dispute, both parties appear to have put self-interest before making a reasonable attempt to settle the dispute without litigation. Agreement of final account sums can result in dispute particularly where there are cost and time over-runs.

These disputes often arise over the valuation and agreement of entitlement to variations. In the case of *St Austell v Dawnus*[89] there were 115 variations disputed within the final account submission and the final account discussions were protracted and did not progress smoothly. Matters were not helped by a change of contract administrator whose replacement was not openly accepted by the contractor. Issues also arise in agreeing entitlement to an Extension of Time when the works are completed after the agreed contract completion date. In construction, late delivery brings costs and it is often who bears the burden of these costs that lead to dispute, particularly where there are liquidated damages that can be applied. One of the major recent cases relating to this is *City Inn v Shepherd Construction*[90] and the matter is also raised in the case of *Balfour Beatty v Shepherd Construction.*[91]

Another factor that has the potential to impact on disputes is the complexity of the contractual arrangements. This is particularly so

---

[89] St. Austell Printing Co. Ltd v Dawnus Construction Holdings Ltd [2015] EWHC 96 (TCC)

[90] City Inn Ltd v Shepherd Construction Ltd [2010] ScotCS CSIH_68

[91] Balfour Beatty Engineering Services (HY) Ltd v Shepherd Construction Ltd [2009] EWHC 2218 TCC, 127 Con LR 110

when contractors are passing on risk to the supply chain. There can be references made to main contract documents and provisions which can lead to disputes arising over the proper construction of the subcontract[92]. The complexity of the arrangement causing dispute is also highlighted in the case of *Hyder v Carillion*[93] where there was a mechanism in the contract for work being undertaken on a lump sum basis and time related charges for work not covered by the lump sum price. The main contract was based on a target cost and disputes arose over the build-up to the fee claimed by Hyder in relation to the target cost. Framework contracts are also not without their problems. In the case of *Amec v Thames Water*[94] there was an encompassing framework agreement in place between the parties and a dispute arose over payment which resulted in a further dispute as to whether it was the terms of the works order or the framework agreement that were relevant to the payment issues.

3.9. The construction industry and alternative dispute resolution

Since the late 1980s, it had been apparent that conventional litigation was too cumbersome, slow and expensive for certain types of disputes, particularly construction disputes. It was due to this that ADR was developed for the resolution of disputes in this sector (McGeorge et al, 2007). The courts have also proven keen to promote ADR during the early stages of litigation proceedings, particularly when litigation costs would be likely to exceed the amount under dispute[95]. This was the case in *Egan v Motor Services (Bath) Ltd* [90] in which the Court recognised that the parties had unreasonably spent approximately £100,000 on litigation when the sum in dispute was only

---

[92] Bovis Lend Lease Ltd v Cofely Engineering Services [2009] EWHC 1120

[93] Hyder Consulting (UK) Ltd v Carillion Construction Ltd [2011] EWHC 1810 (TCC)

[94] AMEC Group Ltd v Thames Water Utilities Ltd [2010] EWHC 419 (TCC)

[95] AMEC Group Ltd v Thames Water Utilities Ltd [2010] EWHC 419 (TCC)

£6,000. It is due to the reduced costs and time involved in ADR that it is increasingly used to resolve construction disputes. Additionally, parties tend to prefer ADR because they perceive it to be more creative and focused on the objective of problem-solving than litigation, which is based on the adversarial, rigid 'win-lose' outcome (Stipanovich,2004). It is also due to this that standard construction contracts now typically feature adjudication provisions for the resolution of disputes. This was primarily prompted by the Latham Report's recommendation for the inclusion of such provisions in standard form construction contracts[96].

The construction industry is prone to disputes due to the complexity of its contacts involving important deadlines and various parties, with huge financial sums at stake]. The submission of construction disputes to litigation in the 1980s resulted in many time-consuming and extremely expensive trials (Hensler,2003).

The practical and economic inefficiencies involved in litigating such disputes resulted in a shift toward ADR. Accordingly, the courts have embraced the resolution of construction disputes through ADR: 'the judiciary spares not effort to divert such cases to any available form of alternative dispute resolution' (Latham, 2004). A 2020 UK construction industry survey highlighted the three most prevalent issues in construction disputes as delays, payment and changes to the scope of works, with varying site conditions and design identified as the next major categories (Groton, 2020). These findings are consistent with those of a 2019 survey of legal professionals involved in litigation at the Technology and Construction Courts in England (Mix, 2020).

Although a majority of construction claims are settled by negotiation, many do become disputes requiring resolution. Such disputes have

[96] Egan v Motor Services (Bath) Ltd [2007] EWCA Civ 1002

been described as 'prolongation and aggression', which feed on each other making dispute resolution in the industry 'conspicuously exhausting of time, energy, money and spirit' (Steen, 2004). Traditionally, such resolution would have been by either arbitration or litigation. However, disillusionment with these processes and a growing need to change have long been recognised by many in the construction industry and the legal profession.

3.10. Summary

This chapter has reviewed the nature of construction disputes, the causes of the disputes and their effects. it is important to understand that issue related to disputes can often jeopardize any given project and prevent the success of project for all parties involved. Understanding the definition of dispute is based upon its purpose and its place. Disputes can arise in various forms and reasons. Most disputes in commerce generally and in construction in particular arise from some form of uncertainty. The disputes may well be disguised but all will involve either a conflict of ideas, beliefs or interests and are most likely to arise where there is some uncertainty. The standard forms of contract such as JCT, FIDIC and NEC also include clauses regarding to dispute resolution. However, Sir Latham in the report "Constructing the Team" stated *"Nevertheless disputes may arise, despite everyone's best efforts to avoid them", negotiating and attempt to prevent disputes at an early stage can alter the path to a less adversarial settlement"*.

References

Akintan, O.A. and Morledge, (2013), Improving the Collaboration between Main Contractors and Subcontractors within Traditional Construction Procurement, Journal of Construction Engineering, Volume 2013, article ID 261236

Al-Hyari, O.H., (2020). Applicability of the 2017 FIDIC Red Book in Civil Law Jurisdictions. Arab Law Quarterly, 1(aop), pp.1-20.

Arbitration Act 1996, s9 (4)

Barlow, J., Cohen, M., Jashapara, A. and Simpson, Y, (1997) Towards Positive Partnering, The Policy Press, Bristol

Batt, P.J. and Purchase, S (2004), Managing collaboration within networks and relationships, Industrial Marketing Management 33 (2004) 169-174

Black, C., Akintoye, A. and Fitzgerald, E (1999), An analysis of success factors and benefits of partnering in construction, International Journal of Project Management 18 (2000) 423-434

Brensen, M. and Marshall, N. (2002), The engineering or evolution of co-operation? A tale of two partnering projects, International Journal of Project Management 20, pp 497-505

Briscoe, G., Dainty, A.R.J. and Millett, S, (2001), Construction supply chain partnerships: skills, knowledge and attitudinal requirements, European Journal of Purchasing & Supply Management 7 (2001) 243-255

Brink, W., 2021. Assessing programme clause changes in the (2017) FIDIC Red Book. Civil Engineering, 29(2), pp.68-69.

Campbell, P (1997) Construction Disputes: Avoidance and Resolution, Whittles Publishing, Caithness.

Cannon, J., Hillebrandt, P.M. and Lansley, P., (2016). The Construction Company in and out of Recession. Springer.

Cotovelea, C.A.M., (2021). DAB/DAAB-A Comparative View between FIDIC 1999/2017 Editions: Part 1-Constitution. Rom. Arb. J., 15, p.80.

Chapman, P.H., (2009). Dispute boards on major infrastructure projects. Proceedings of the Institution of Civil Engineers-Management, Procurement and Law, 162(1), pp.7-16.

Cox, A. and Thompson, I. (1997) 'Fit for purpose' contractual relations: determining a theoretical framework for construction projects, European Journal of Purchasing and Supply Management, Vol 3, No. 3 pp 127-135

Dan Bishop , Alan Felstead , Alison Fuller , Nick Jewson , Lorna Unwin & Konstantinos Kakavelakis (2009) Constructing learning: adversarial and collaborative working in the British construction industry, Journal of Education and Work, 22:4, 243-260,

Department for Business Innovation & Skills, (2013). Quarterly Price and Cost Indices: Commentary IQ2013. London: DBIS.

De Bono, E., (1990). Conflicts: A Better Way to Resolve Them. New York: International Centre for Creative Thinking.

El-Sayegh, S., Ahmad, I., Aljanabi, M., Herzallah, R., Metry, S. and El-Ashwal, O., (2020). Construction disputes in the UAE: Causes and resolution methods. Buildings, 10(10), p.171.

Gerber, P., (2013). Dispute Avoidance Procedures ('DAPs')-The Changing Face of Construction Dispute Management. Gerber, Paula 'Dispute Avoidance Procedures ('DAPs')–The Changing Face of Construction Dispute Management'(2001), 1, pp.122-129.

Groton, J., (1991). Preventing and Resolving Construction Disputes (CPR Legal Program Construction Disputes Committee, Center For Public Resources).

Hellard, R., (1988). Managing Construction Conflict. New York: Longman Higher Education.

Hensler, D.R., (2003). Our courts, ourselves: how the alternative dispute resolution movement is re-shaping our legal system. Penn St. L. Rev., 108, p.165.

Hughes, W., Champion, R. and Murdoch, J., (2015). Construction contracts: law and management. Routledge.

Humphries, P., Matthews, J. and Kumaraswamy, M. (2003), Pre-construction project partnering: from adversarial to collaborative relationships, Supply Chain Management: An International Journal, Vol. 8 Iss 2 pp 166-178

Kale, S and Arditi, D (2001), General contractors' relationships with subcontractors: a strategic asset, Construction Management and Economics, Vol 19, No. 5 pp 541-549

Kaufmann, P.J. and Stern, L.W., (1988). Relational exchange norms, perceptions of unfairness and retained hostility in commercial litigation. Journal of conflict resolution, 32(3), pp.534-552.

Latham, M., (1994). Constructing the Team: Final Report of the Government/ Industry Review of Procurement and Contractual Arrangements in the UK Construction Industry. London: Stationery Office.

Lumbwe, B., (2020). FIDIC 2017 Edition of Contracts-The Repercussions of Defining the Words Claim & Dispute on the Claims and Dispute Referral Procedures. Arbitration: The International Journal of Arbitration, Mediation and Dispute Management, 86(4), pp.447-462.

Mackie, K., Miles, D., & Marsh, W., (2000). Commercial Dispute Resolution. London: Butterworths.

Mahnken, V., (2018). On construction adjudication, the ICC dispute board rules and the dispute board provisions of the 2017 FIDIC conditions of contracts. McGill J. Disp. Resol., 5, p.60.

McGeorge, D., London, K., Love, P., Davis, P., Jefferies, M., Ward, P. and Chesworth, B., (2007). Dispute avoidance and resolution a literature review. CRC for construction innovation rep, 1.

Mix, D.M., (1996). ADR in the construction industry: continuing the development of a more efficient dispute resolution mechanism. Ohio St. J. on Disp. Resol., 12, p.463.

Moore, C., Mosley, D. and Slagle, M. (1992) Partnering: guidelines for win-win project management, Project Management Journal, Vol. 23 No. 1, pp 18-21

Owen, G. and Totterdill, B.W., (2008). Dispute boards: procedures and practice (Vol. 4). Oxford: Thomas Telford.

Purba, H. and Yuri Prastowo, T., (2020). Potential risks occurring in fidic contract construction projects: A literature review. Advance Researches in Civil Engineering, 2(1), pp.1-12.

Riches, J and Dancaster, C (2004) Construction Adjudication (practical construction guide), 2nd Edition, Blackwell Publishing, ISBN 1-4051-0635-2, p. 297

RICS Draft Guidance Note – Comparative construction and engineering contracts, https://consultations.rics.org/consult.ti/comparative.construction/view?objectId=2425044

Safinia, S., (2014). A review on dispute resolution methods in UK construction industry. International Journal of Construction Engineering and Management, 3(4), pp.105-108 Seppala, C.R., (1991). Contractors' Claims under the FIDIC Civil Engineering Contract, Fourth (1987) Edition-I. Int'l Bus. Law., 19, p.395.

Steen, R.H. and MacPherson, R.J., (2000). Resolving construction disputes out of court through ADR. Journal of Property Management, 65(5), pp.58-58.

Steen, R.H., (1994). Five steps to resolving construction disputes—Without litigation. Journal of Management in Engineering, 10(4), pp.19-21.

Stipanowich, T.J., (2004). ADR and the 'Vanishing Trial': the growth and impact of 'Alternative Dispute Resolution'. Journal of Empirical Legal Studies, 1(3), pp.843-912.

Van Langelaar, A., (2015). Dispute Boards-Dispute Avoidance Role, Part 1: dispute boards. Civil Engineering= Siviele Ingenieurswese, 2015(1), pp.69-74.

Wood, G.D. and Ellis, R.C.T., (2005), Main contractor experiences of partnering relationships on UK construction projects, Construction Management and Economics 23 (3), pp 317-32

Case Law

AMEC Group Ltd v Thames Water Utilities Ltd [2010] EWHC 419 (TCC)

Balfour Beatty Engineering Services (HY) Ltd v Shepherd Construction Ltd [2009] EWHC 2218 TCC, 127 Con LR 110

Bovis Lend Lease Ltd v Cofely Engineering Services [2009] EWHC 1120

City Inn Ltd v Shepherd Construction Ltd [2010] ScotCS CSIH_68

Egan v Motor Services (Bath) Ltd [2007] EWCA Civ 1002

Ellerine Brothers v Klinger [1982] 1 WLR 1375.

Fastrack Contractors Ltd v Morrison Construction Ltd [2000] BLR 168

Hayter v Nelson Home Insurance [1990] 2 LR 265 per Saville J.

Hyder Consulting (UK) Ltd v Carillion Construction Ltd [2011] EWHC 1810 (TCC)

St. Austell Printing Co. Ltd v Dawnus Construction Holdings Ltd [2015] EWHC 96 (TCC)

Chapter Four: Time-Related Disputes in the Construction Industry

4.1 Introduction

This chapter examines time-related disputes, and the issues that they give rise to, given that they are amongst the most common forms of construction disputes. The purpose of this chapter is to explore how construction disputes should be prevented rather than responded to, in order to avoid the need for dispute resolution in the first place.

4.2. Disputes in relation to time delays: Specific issues

As has been recognised, construction projects are most commonly linked to the phrase 'time is money', due to the fact that they involve extremely high costs (Chassiakos & Sakellaropoulos, 2005). The main aim of employers in construction projects is to ensure the project's timely completion. Time completion enables employers to maximise their returns on their investments, and to achieve minimal cost expenditure for time-related overheads (Mahmoud-Jouini et al, 2004). Thus, time in construction projects is directly linked to money, and vice versa. The duration of construction contracts has a direct impact on their profitability, and affects the interests of all parties involved in the project (Majid & McCaffer, 1998).

It is due to the importance of time in construction projects that most standard forms of contract contain provisions relating to delays that have been caused by the contractor, the owner, or those that are beyond either party's control (Burr, 2016). Contract provisions also provide a basis for the employer's or owner's recovery of liquidated damages from the contractor, if there is failure on his part to complete the project on time. This highlights that liquidated damages play a key role in time-related disputes, in that they enable employers to recover a specific sum for each week that a culpable delay occurs (Eggleston, 2009).

It is typically the case that parties cannot settle delay-related claims in a manner that is amicable, which can cause costly, expensive disputes (NG et al, 2004). Thus, delay claims are a prominent source of construction disputes, and have proven notoriously taxing to resolve. Accordingly, tribunals and courts play a primary role in resolving time-related disputes and claims in the construction industry.

Although standard form contracts seek to avoid such disputes, and despite the existence of principles of best practice within construction contract programmes, most construction projects suffer delays (Trauner et al, 2017). This highlights that such disputes are a key issue relating to dispute resolution in the construction industry.

4.3. Time notice clauses

As of recent, the construction industry has suffered major costs due to disputes arising from notice requirement clauses. Such disputes and claims could have been avoided if due diligence had been exercised by the parties when they submitted the necessary notices. However, it is often the case that contractors rely on promissory estoppel, unconscionability, or waiver, as opposed to attaining strict compliance with provisions relating to notice. Ultimately, time clauses require the contract administrator to comply with the timeline that is contained in the contract, meaning that administrators play a vital role in ensuring the timely completion of construction projects.

Notice clauses provide contractors with the right to claim for time extensions, although the courts have traditionally interpreted them in a narrow manner (Walsh, 2017). It has indeed been found that it is taxing to predict whether or not a court will enforce a notice clause, because the courts adopt a context-specific approach. This highlights the importance of complying with time notice clauses, given that non-compliance could prove fatal to a party's claim.

Under the common law approach, time stipulations are categorised as essential terms, which means that non-compliance with a due date creates the right to terminate the contract, and recover damages. This further highlights the central importance of time in construction projects, as well as construction disputes. In contrast, courts of equity tend to adopt a less strict approach towards time stipulations, because they differentiate between form and substance, and generally state that "performance on time is not essential if the substance of the contract could be carried out and the promisee adequately compensated for loss or damage caused by the promisor's breach" (Halsbury, 2008). However, there is a potential that time is considered to be of the essence in the event that the parties have explicitly agreed as such, or when the courts consider it reasonable to imply this under the circumstances (*Ciavarella v Balmer* (1983) 57 ALJR 632, para.634). In the 21st century, it is generally the case that equity prevails, meaning that time will only be considered of the essence if the parties have expressly agreed as such, or where this can be reasonably implied.

Time limitation clauses are a form of exclusion clause; thus, they operate for a particular party's benefit (*Suisse Atlantique Société d'Armement Maritime SA v NV Rotterdamsche Kolen Centrale* [1967] 1 AC 361). Their determination is made by appeal to the parties' intentions as illustrated in the contractual terms (Sydney Corp v West (1965) 114 CLR, para.481).

Case law shows that time limitation clauses are typically interpreted strictly against the party whom they seek to favour (*Tropican Contractors Pte Ltd v Lojan Properties Pte Ltd* [1989] 3 MLJ 216).

4.4. Extension of time disputes: Common law

In the event that a dispute regarding a specific contract clause arises, the courts attempt to construe the clause so as to give effect to it. The courts in England and Wales prefer an objective approach, which involves an objective assessment of what was intended by the parties (Stone, 2011). If the clause is worded ambiguously, the court will seek further evidence that may indicate the intentions of the parties, such as, for example, trade customs (*Robertson v Jackson* [1845] 2 CB 412). Extrinsic evidence may also be referred to as a foundation for filling in any gaps that exist in the contract, although such evidence can only be admitted for the purposes of clarifying the contract, not for varying it (*Allen v Pink* [1838] 4 M&W 140).

It is apparent that the court sin England and Wales prefer the purposive commercial approach, which involves consideration and interpretation of the contract terms within its context so as to be accurately understood. This suggests that litigation is a particularly effective form of dispute resolution for such disputes, because it promotes certainty and predictability in terms of outcome. Preference for the purposive approach was expressed in *Reardon Smith-Line v Hansen-Tangen* ([1976] 1 WLR 989), in which it was determined by Wilberforce LJ that the court needed to be placed in the same "factual matrix" as the parties at the time that they established the contract. This seeks to give effect to the parties' intentions, as opposed to imposing some other presumption of what the courts consider should have been the case. Such an approach is provoked by the fact that there is a lack of an explicit concept of good faith under English contract law. This essentially means that the parties are free to pursue their own goals and interests when negotiating contracts. Good faith is generally considered to be inappropriate by the English courts, because it is extremely subjective and is too vague to be applied to contractual relations. Although there are cases in which the courts have referred to principles such as "reasonable standard of conduct", as well as "fair dealing" (*Yam Seng v international Trade Corporation* [2013] EWHC 111 (QB): para.115), these are extremely context-specific.

4.5. Extension of time disputes: The FIDIC silver and red books

The FIDIC Silver Book may be utilised when the employer states that the contractor must assume absolute responsibility for the construction and design of a project. This minimises the involvement of the employer, who will only engage with the project in order to oversee compliance. This means that the contractor is subject to a significantly higher level of risk that under other standard contract forms (Le Goff, 2000)). It is for this reason that the employer will pay a premium fee in order to reflect such increased risk, which also maximises certainty in relation to the project's time and final price.

The FIDIC Silver Book does, however, provide contractors with the right of relief by permitting an extension of time under specific conditions. Such conditions are outlined in Sub-Clause 8.4, and involve extensions due to a variation, for a delay cause, or for any delay that has been caused by or is attributable to the employer.

The express right to a time extension is offered in a range of circumstances, such as testing (Sub-Clause 7.4), right of access to the project site (Sub-Clause 2.1), delays that have been caused by authorities (Sub-Clause 8.5), and adjustments due to legislative changes (Sub-Clause 13.7). It is important to point out that unforeseeable conditions do not give rise to the right to relief, such as adverse ground or weather conditions, indicating the contractor's increased assumption of risk under the FIDIC Silver Book. Indeed, it is explicitly stated under Sub-Clause 4.12 that the contractor, unless it has been otherwise stipulated in the contract, "is deemed to have obtained al necessary information as to risks, contingencies and other circumstances which may influence or affect the works".

It is of primary importance that the contractor and the employer, at the commencement of the claim process, agree upon the main issues of the claim, as well as the employer's entitlement assessment and determination. This is due to the fact that no party's interests will be promoted if a contractor is required to expend large periods of time, effort and expenses in preparing extension of time claims, only for the employer to reject the methodology or approach that he has adopted. This places emphasis on the need for appropriate co-operation and planning between the employer and the contractor before an extension of time claim is submitted. Thus, further disputes can be avoided. This is also reflected I Sub-Clause 1.3 of the FIDIC Silver Books, which states that "approvals, certifications, consents and determinations shall not be unreasonably withheld or delayed" on the part of the employer. Despite this, it has been found that evaluations of claims made by employers can take up to several months (Gibson, 2008).

Employers will tend to make "requests for further necessary particulars" under the authority of Sub-Clause 20.1 so as to cause illegitimate delays in evaluations of entitlement to extension of time. In this context, the FIDIC Silver Book is lacking, because it does not effectively protect against bad faith on the part of employers. The abovementioned problem is further aggravated by the lack of guidance in the FIDIC Silver Book on how employers are required to evaluate and determine the entitlement of contractors to an extension of time.

It is merely stated in Sub-Clause 3.5 that the employer must consult with the contractor and attempt to reach an agreement, and the failure to do so enables the employer to make a "fair determination in accordance with the contract". This provision is considerably vague, and fails to offer sufficient safeguards that prevent employers from bad faith delays of evaluations of extension of time claims. Thus, the FIDIC Silver Book could be considered lacking in this respect, because it does not ensure that employers do not delay claims due to bad faith, which increases the potential for disputes. This also provokes further delays, particularly if the dispute is to be sent to a form of dispute resolution.

In 2017, the second edition of the FIDIC Red Book was published, which mainly preserves the structure of the previous 1999 edition, but adopts a range of updates and improvements. A key aim of the 2017 was to offer a more effective allocation of risk, as well as to increase the role of project management, which would contribute to decreased disputes. Indeed, the underlying objective of the second edition has been to reduce construction disputes, which in turn increases the timely and successful completion of construction projects (Fawzy et al, 2018). Particular focus in this respect has been placed on extension of time evaluation and entitlement procedure. It is not difficult to understand why the 2017 edition of the FIDIC Red Book attempted to improve the mechanisms for extension of time claims. It has been widely recognised that such claims are amongst the most frequent causes of construction disputes (Kelsey & Punwar, 2017).

Accordingly, the 2017 FIDIC Red Book implemented a range of amendments to the sub-clauses on extension of time claims. A key amendment was the responsibilities regarding the placing, substantiation, and evaluation of claims for extension of time. Sub-Clause 8.4 on advance warning requires that all parties warn each other of any actual or expected event that could potentially impact the work's performance, or delay the construction project. This same provision imposes the duty to seek a mitigation or avoidance in relation to the impact of such events. However, this has no effect on

Sub-Clause 20.2.1 on notice of claim, which means that the contractor is still under the duty to notify an extension of time within 28 days.

Following notification, the FIDIC Red Book offers detailed guidance on what is required to be submitted so as to substantiate a claim, which is clear advantage that the FIDIC Red Book has when compared to the FIDIC Silver Book. This is because the latter lacks such detail, which increases the potential for disputes, further delays, and the need to resort to dispute resolution. This also demonstrates that effective guidance on such matters is key to minimising the potential for disputes in construction contracts. Finally, more detailed guidance prevents employers from delaying evaluations of claims in bad faith, which further contributes to reducing the potential for disputes.

4.6. Time delays and damages

Typically, a claim for extension of time is followed by a claim for cost, which has as its key purpose the recovery of additional costs resulting from the performance of work after the contract completion date (Ndekugri et al, 2008). In order for a contractor to recover such costs, three conditions must be satisfied: (a) demonstrate the cause of the delay impacted the critical path of the programme, (b) the cause of the delay must be excusable according to the contract, subject to an express or an implied term, (c) the delay cause must be compensable.

A field of construction law that has given rise to significant debate is delay analysis, problems with which can increase the potential for disputes. It is common for construction projects to be delayed, which can give rise to differing conclusions depending on the method of analysis used to evaluate the impact of a delay (Arditi & Pattanakitchamroon, 2006). Accordingly, parties tend to employ delay experts to conduct such evaluations. However, a problem with this is that there is no actual consensus on the preferred method for analysing delays. The choice of method is generally dependent on the contractual, factual and legal issues involved in any specific construction project (Braimah, 2013). The fact that these elements tend to be unique to the particular project exacerbates the negative implications of the lack of a common stance on delay analysis. This, in turn, can cause greater disputes in such circumstances. In determining who bears the responsibility for a particular delay, there is a need to distinguish between culpable and excusable delay.

Although in-depth analysis of these elements is beyond the scope and purpose of this study, it is worth noting that culpable delay arises from a contractor delay event, while an excusable delay arises from an employer delay event (Schumacher, 1995). This emphasises the need to identify and distinguish effectively between employer and contractor delay events.

However, it has been noted that establishing such a distinction is not always easy, given the highly complex relationship between events (Al-Azad et al, 2019). This further demonstrates the specific characteristics of such issues, which can increase the potential for disputes.

A further distinction has been established between retrospective and prospective delay analysis. A key judgement in this respect is *Fluor v Shanghai Zhenhua Heavy Industry Co Ltd* ([2018] EWHC 1 (TCC)), in which a construction project was for the construction of wind turbine generators. The structures for the wind turbine generators had been delivered, and defects were found in the structure welds, which delayed the completion of the project, and incurred increased costs arising from the need to repair the defects. The court had to determine the critical path before and after the defects were discovered, as well as whether it was necessary to adopt a prospective or retrospective approach towards delay analysis. Prospective delay analysis features theoretical evaluation of criticality, and the probably effect of the delay on the project's progress and completion, on the basis of what was known at that specific time. It is because of its forward-looking approach that such a method is most commonly applied by contractors to indicate extension of time due as a consequence of employer delay events (Ghimire & Mishra, 2019).

In contrast, retrospective analysis involves analysis of subsequent events, and other conditions that impact the project's progress, so as to identify the actual impact of any delays on the construction project, as well as whether they actually delayed the completion of the project (Hallock & Mehta, 2007). This involves factual analysis, with evaluation of the project's overall progress. The issue concerning which approach is to be adopted is central to extension of time claim outcomes.

Although the courts in different jurisdictions adopt different approaches, they typically presume that if prospective and retrospective analysis is conducted accurately, they will create the same result (*Walter Lilly & Co Ltd v Mackay* [2012] EWHC 1773 (TCC)). However, this is not necessarily the case, because retrospective delay analysis focuses on what actually occurred, while prospective delay analysis is more predictive.

In *Fluor*, the court assessed which method is preferable, and ultimately expressed preference for prospective analysis in the context of extension of time claims. Practically, this is an appropriate approach, because it is beneficial for extension of time assessments to be dealt with as soon as possible. This also reduces the potential for delays, and further disputes. Thus, it is possible to argue that the courts have proven both willing and able to adopt an appropriate approach towards delay analysis. It is worth noting that the court in *Fluor* also emphasised the need to conduct at least some form of retrospective analysis in relation to the facts.

This embodies well-established principles and rules regarding damages assessment in cases of breach of contract. Thus, this particular judgement arguably reflects the reality of construction time disputes, and demonstrates that the courts are able to adopt an approach towards such disputes. Thus, it is not always the case that alternative forms of dispute resolution are suitable for all construction disputes.

4.7. Summary

Construction projects are often linked to the phrase 'time is money' because they involve extremely high costs. This chapter has examined the example of time-related disputes, given that they are a particularly common form of construction dispute and emphasise the importance of time in construction projects. This chapter has assessed the applicable principles, the implications of such disputes, and how they are dealt with.

References

Al-Azad, N., Enegbuma, W.I., Bamgbade, J.A. and Ohueri, C.C., (2019), November. Influencing factors in extension of time claims. Australasian Universities Building Education Association Conference (Vol. 43, pp. 70-85).

Arditi, D. and Pattanakitchamroon, T., (2006). Selecting a delay analysis method in resolving construction claims. International Journal of project management, 24(2), pp.145-155.

Braimah, N., (2013). Construction delay analysis techniques—A review of application issues and improvement needs. Buildings, 3(3), pp.506-531.

Burr, A., (2016). Delay and disruption in construction contracts. Oxford: Routledge.

Chassiakos, A.P. and Sakellaropoulos, S.P., (2005). Time-cost optimization of construction projects with generalized activity constraints. Journal of Construction Engineering and Management, 131(10), pp.1115-1124.

Eggleston, B., (2009). Liquidated damages and extensions of time: In construction contracts. (3rd edn). London: John Wiley.

Fawzy, S.A., El-Adaway, I.H., Perreau-Saussine, L., Wahad, M.S.A. and Hamed, T.H., (2018). Claims for Extension of Time and Additional Payment under Common Law FIDIC: Civil Law Analysis. Journal of legal affairs and dispute resolution in engineering and construction, 10(4).

Ghimire, S. and Mishra, A.K., (2019). Comparative Study of Prospective Delay Analysis Techniques (DATs). Saudi J Civ Eng, 3(5), pp.84-95.

Gibson, R., (2008). Construction delays: Extensions of time and prolongation claims. Oxford: Routledge.

Kelsey, S. and Punwar, P., (2017). Variations and the Resolution of Disputes under the FIDIC Red Books. BCDR International Arbitration Review, 4(1).

Hallock, BE & and Mehta, P.M., (2007). The Great Debate-TIA vs WINDOWS: A Better Path for Retrospective Delay Analysis?. AACE International Transactions, p.CD41.

Halsbury, H.S., (2008). Halsbury's Laws of Australia. Sydney: Butterworths.

Le Goff, P., 2000. A new standard for international turnkey contracts: The FIDIC Silver book. Int'l Bus. LJ, p.151.

Mahmoud-Jouini, S.B., Midler, C. and Garel, G., (2004). Time-to-market vs. time-to-delivery: Managing speed in Engineering, Procurement and Construction projects. International Journal of Project Management, 22(5), pp.359-367.

Majid, M.A. and McCaffer, R., (1998). Factors of non-excusable delays that influence contractors' performance. Journal of management in engineering, 14(3), pp.42-49.

Ndekugri, I., Braimah, N. and Gameson, R., (2008). Delay analysis within construction contracting organizations. Journal of construction engineering and management, 134(9), pp.692-700.

Ng, S.T., Skitmore, M., Deng, M.Z.M. and Nadeem, A., (2004). Improving existing delay analysis techniques for the establishment of delay liabilities. Construction Innovation, 4(1), pp.3-17.

Schumacher, L., (1995). Quantifying and apportioning delay on construction projects. Cost engineering, 37(2), p.11.

Stone, R., (2011). The Modern Law of Contract. (9th edn). Oxford: Routledge.

Trauner, TJ., S Lowe, MF Nagata & WA Manginelli, (2017). Construction delays. London: Elsevier.

Walsh, K.P., (2017). Identifying and mitigating the risks created by problematic clauses in construction contracts. Journal of Legal Affairs and Dispute Resolution in Engineering and Construction, 9(3), p.03717001.

Case Law

Allen v Pink [1838] 4 M&W 140).

Ciavarella v Balmer (1983) 57 ALJR 632, para.634)

Fluor v Shanghai Zhenhua Heavy Industry Co Ltd ([2018] EWHC 1 (TCC)),

Reardon Smith-Line v Hansen-Tangen ([1976] 1 WLR 989),

Robertson v Jackson [1845] 2 CB 412).

Suisse Atlantique Société d'Armement Maritime SA v NV Rotterdamsche Kolen Centrale [1967] 1 AC 361).

Sydney Corp v West (1965) 114 CLR, para.481).

Tropican Contractors Pte Ltd v Lojan Properties Pte Ltd [1989] 3 MLJ 216).

Walter Lilly & Co Ltd v Mackay [2012] EWHC 1773 (TCC)).

Yam Seng v international Trade Corporation [2013] EWHC 111 (QB): para.115)

Chapter Five: The Evolving Role of Arbitration, Adjudication and the Technology and Construction Court

5.1 Introduction

This chapter considers the extent to which arbitration and adjudication apply to construction disputes and how this has been approached from a legal perspective. This requires that focus be placed on key legislative instruments and the Technology and Construction Court's (TCC) role in and approach to resolving construction disputes.

5.2. Evaluation of arbitration for construction disputes

The effectiveness of arbitration for construction disputes is multi-dimensional, and consists of time, costs and the award's quality. These three key dimensions can be examined on a normative or an objective basis. The cost and time of construction arbitration can be objectively assessed by calculating the actual time that it takes, and the costs that the parties have incurred in resolving the dispute. Such issues can also be assessed normatively, by comparing the actual cost and time against some specific set standard, such as the expected cost and time, or the reasonableness of the cost and time when compared to like disputes. For example, some studies have found that arbitrations that are resolved by multi-member arbitral tribunals and sole arbitrators should not take more than 6 months (Fortese & Hemmi, 2015). However, other studies have found that arbitration is more expensive and time-consuming than litigation and other methods of dispute resolution (Besaiso et al, 2018). It is due to this that arbitration has lost popularity in construction disputes, particularly when compared to other forms of dispute resolution. This is perplexing, given that arbitration was developed in order to remedy the problems surrounding litigation, such as high costs and time delays.

There is a generally emerging notion that the cost and time of arbitration is unreasonable when it is found to exceed or be equal to that involved in resolving like disputes through litigation (Harmon, 2003). Therefore, when considered normatively and objectively, time and cost as measures of efficiency are referred to as time efficiency and cost effectiveness. The objective assessments of the award's quality also include the type of the awards as indicated in statutory instruments. However, from a normative perspective, such quality also involves the extent to which the disputing parties are cooperative, particularly in terms of accepting or challenging the award, and their willingness to preserve relationships once the dispute has been resolved.

Existing literature suggests that very few construction disputes are successfully resolved by arbitration (Lee et al, 2016). However, such studies contribute little attention to the reasons as to why this may be the case. Of the few studies that actually embarked upon such a task, they found that arbitral effectiveness was a key cause (Abwunza, 2020).

More recently however, it has been found that there are four key issues that impact the effectiveness of arbitration for construction disputes – the complexity of the dispute, the competence of the tribunal, the manner in which evidence is presented, and the effectiveness of multi-member tribunals (Abwunza et al, 2019).

Complex disputes can often result in long and delayed procedures that are not dissimilar to those utilised in litigation, which undermines the distinction between arbitration and litigation. Complexities can result from the nature of the dispute, the number of parties involved, and the number of contracts concerned. The dispute may require that contracts be interpreted, so as to determine the legal or contractual basis of the issues that are under dispute. A dispute may also become more complex when there are many parties involved, or many contracts, which can give rise to challenges relating to jurisdiction. Thus, a construction dispute may require many sittings in order to address such issues.

A further issue relates to arbitrator competence. This may arise from poor skill base or limited knowledge. In the context of knowledge, arbitrators that lack specialisation in the specific subject matter of the dispute will be likely to encounter difficulties in understanding the technical characteristics of the dispute (Jahren & Dammeier, 1990). This can give rise to the need for expensive experts to assist them in deconstructing and understanding the dispute.

Studies show that arbitrators who knowledge of the relevant legal issues, and the practice of arbitration will also require legal assistance in order to minimise the granting of an award that may later become unenforceable. In the context of skills who lack functional skills may experience difficulties in accurately or effectively identifying and assessing the issues at dispute, which can hinder a resolution. Such problems can result in power imbalances going unnoticed, and the inability of arbitrators to deal with the parties' underlying emotions and values. All of these issues can undermine the arbitration process, rendering it less effective for construction disputes. It has also been found that multi-member tribunals can undermine the effectiveness of arbitration for construction disputes. They may, for example, find it difficult to synchronise time to attend hearings. They may also take longer to consider the reasons for an award, which results in extra costs and time delays. Finally, the presentation of evidence can also impact the effectiveness of arbitration for construction disputes.

This is most apparent in the context of poor or insufficient documentation, which can cause delays in the proceedings, and increase the costs of the process. This is because extra time will be required to search through a large volume of documents in order to locate the relevant information. It is therefore evident that there are a range of potential factors that could cause arbitration to be ineffective for construction disputes. This is primarily due to the impact of such factors on time and cost, which are vital to construction projects.

5.3. Adjudication

It was not until the Latham Report that adjudication became a statutory requirement in the UK, to be included within all construction contracts (HGCRA 1996, ss. 104, 105). Thus, construction contracts are now required to adequately provide for adjudication. The HGCRA 1996 clearly stipulates such requirements. However, should a construction contract fail to achieve full or partial compliance with such requirements, then the Scheme for Construction Contracts 1998 (SCC 1998) is to be used in order to fill any gaps. The aggressive approach towards adjudication in the UK is considered necessary in order to avoid expensive and time-consuming disputes from negatively impacting construction projects (Gould & Linneman, 2008). Accordingly, the adjudicator is required to resolve an issue presented to him within 28 days, unless the parties have agreed upon a later date in accordance with section 19(b) or (c) SCC 1998.

The aim of adjudication is not to provide a final, but rather a fast and temporary resolution of disputes. It seeks to address cashflow problems that arise from litigation and arbitration, which can take such a great amount of time and resources that they jeopardise the construction project (*Macob Civil Engineering Ltd v Morrison Construction Ltd* [1999] BLR 93). However, adjudication is considered by some to be similar to arbitration in that it features a set procedure, as set out in the HGCRA 1996 and the SCC 1998 (Ezurmendia & Gonzalez, 2021). As has been recognised already, adjudication involves the submission of a dispute to a third party (the adjudicator) for an interim decision, which has binding effect until the final resolution of the dispute through arbitration or litigation. However, it is important to point out that the vast majority of disputes sent to adjudication do not proceed to litigation or arbitration, as the parties tend to accept the adjudicator's decision as final (Salmon, 2007).

The adjudicator has a rather limited time period within which he must make a decision. This means that the cost of adjudication is generally lower when compared to arbitration, precisely because of the shorter timeframe (Kennedy, 2008). A further benefit of adjudication is that it ensures confidentiality, unless judicial intervention is required to enforce the decision.

Overall, adjudication is a relatively less formal procedure than litigation or arbitration, which the parties agree to, meaning that they will be more likely to accept the adjudicator's decision. The rules and principles of natural justice are applicable to adjudication, meaning that the adjudicator must act in an impartial and fair manner (Merrill, 2018). Although such requirements are also present in arbitration, the key difference between arbitration and adjudication in this respect is that there is a set timescale for the adjudicator to make a decision. Additionally, the parties must cover their own costs, unless they have agreed otherwise. Another significant distinction between arbitration and adjudication is that arbitral awards are final and binding, and can only be challenged on limited grounds (Hodges, 2000). In contrast, adjudication is only binding until the dispute has been resolved through litigation or arbitration (HGCRA 1996, s.108(3)). However, as has been recognised above, the majority of adjudication outcomes are accepted by the parties and therefore rarely proceed to arbitration or litigation.

It is important to emphasise that the main purpose of adjudication (the speedy and cheap resolution of disputes to ensure cashflow) is maintained throughout the construction contract. It is even possible for adjudication to be conducted following the practical completion of the project. In *Pepper v Hart* ([1993] AC 593, Dyson LJ, para.634), it was ruled that adjudication may be conducted "at any time", even long after the practical completion of a project. The use of the term 'at any time' was deemed important to the court, else it would be possible "for a party bent on avoiding adjudication to insert a term which would allow notice to be given within an unreasonably narrow window", which could not be reasonably accepted or permitted (House of Lords, 1996, Lord Lucas, col.1344).

The UK courts have recognised some controversy surrounding this principle, although it has been confirmed that:

> *"there may be times, even at such a late stage, where it is desirable to have a quick and cheap procedure that can produce an effective temporary decision, particularly since this will not prevent parties from seeking a permanent decision through arbitration or the courts" (Connex South Eastern Ltd v M J Building Services Group plc* [2005] EWCA Civ 193, Dyson LJ, para.36).

Section 108(2)(e-f) HGCRA 1996 states that a construction contract must provide that the adjudicator be subject to the duty to act in an impartial manner, and that the contract must authorise the adjudicator to take the initiative in identifying the relevant facts and legal principles.

In *Macob Civil Engineering Ltd v Morrison Construction Ltd.* ([1999] BLR 93: para.29), Dyson LJ emphasised that the adjudicator has rather broad discretion in determining the procedure, can "conduct an entirely inquisitorial process…[and]…may invite representations from the parties".

Furthermore, in *Costain Ltd v Strathclyde Builders Ltd* ([2004] SLT 102), Drummond LJ clarified the rules of natural justice that are applicable to adjudication, as well as the general conduct of the adjudicator: primarily that of adjudicator impartiality. This is further illustrated in *Discain Project Services Ltd. v. Opecprime Development Ltd.* ([2001] BLR 285 TCC), in which the adjudicator had attempted to record conversations between himself and the parties, but had failed to produce a complete record of such conversations. One of the parties had had several conversations with the adjudicator in private, which had not been recorded. The court ruled that the adjudicator's conduct was such that it could objectively be argued that he was potentially biased. It was upon this basis that the decision of the adjudicator was set aside, and the court emphasised that it would "decline to enforce contracts tainted by illegality…[or]…enforce a decision reached after substantial breach of the rules of natural justice" (Discain, Bowsher QC: para.22). Additionally, in *Balfour Beatty Construction Ltd v The London Borough of Lambeth* ([2002] EWHC 597 (TCC)), the adjudicator had established a formula in order to make sense of the material, although he failed to inform the parties of this, or allow them to comment on its suitability. The court ruled that the adjudicator had failed to act in a sufficiently fair manner. This demonstrates that adjudication does not evade the rules of natural justice that are applied to other forms of dispute resolution – namely, arbitration and litigation. This seeks to maintain the legitimacy of this form of dispute resolution, and its ability to promote fair and just outcomes.

Since the statutory introduction of adjudication, the courts have proven willing to give effect to adjudicators' decisions, even in the event that they contain errors of fact and law. In Ballast plc v The *Burrell Co (Construction Management) Ltd* ([2002] SC 279), the adjudicator had refused to make a decision on the dispute, due to concerns that the parties had failed to strictly observe the terms of the JCT standard form of contract on dealing with third parties, as well as each other. The court determined that the adjudicator was under a legal obligation to determine a dispute brought to him in cases in which the dispute fell within his jurisdiction. Thus, the adjudicator's failure to make a judgement in this case meant that he had committed an error of law, and his (non)decision was accordingly null.

In *Bouygues UK Ltd v Dahl-Jensen UK Ltd* ([2000] BLR 49), the adjudicator had erroneously made a net award for the value of £200,000 in favour of one of the disputing parties, when in fact a lesser sum should have been awarded to the other party. Both the parties and the adjudicator readily recognised the error.

Dyson LJ applied the reasoning in *Nikko Hotels (UK) Ltd v MEPC Plc* ([1991] 2 EGLR 103), in reasoning that the adjudicator had answered the correct question in the wrong manner, with the result that the decision was binding. Had the adjudicator attempted to answer the incorrect question, this would have nullified his decision. Thus, case law demonstrates that the courts will uphold the decisions of adjudicators in all but the most serious of circumstances. This arguably represents the courts' reluctance to interfere in the adjudication process and outcome, thus maintaining the distinction between adjudication and litigation.

5.4. Evaluation of adjudication as a hybrid system

In *Campbell v Edwards* ([1976] 1 WLR 403: para.408), Denning LJ established a distinction between arbitration and expert determination of disputes. Depending on the remit of the expert, there is no general requirement that the rules of natural justice be followed, or that the principles of procedural fairness and due process be observed (*Owen Pell Ltd v Bindi (London) Ltd* [2008] EWHC 1420 (TCC): para.23). Adjudication may be identified as a compromise between expert determination and arbitration. It is a form of hybrid form of ADR, which incorporates components of both expert determination and arbitration, without the finality of decision-making that they impose. The courts have in fact suggested that adjudication is slightly closer to arbitration than expert determination on the ADR spectrum (*Deko Scotland Ltd v Edinburgh Royal Joint Venture & Others* [2003] SLT 727, Drummond L: para.9).

The distinction between arbitral and expert determination may have less significance in practice when considered in the context of adjudication (identified in *Campbell v Edwards* [1976] 1 WLR 403; *Glencot Development & Design Ltd v Ben Barrett & Son (Contractors) Ltd* [2001] EWHC 15 (TCC)). This is because the statutory adjudication scheme necessitates that the adjudicator has regard to the relevant information that has been submitted by the parties and to make available to them any information that he has taken into account when making a decision. To that extent, adjudication appears to be more closely linked to arbitration than expert determination (Gaitskell, 2007). However, section 108(2)(f) HGCRA 1996 has the effect of rebalancing adjudication, pressing it towards expert determination. It achieves this by requiring that the adjudicator take the initiative to ascertain the law and the facts necessary to determine the dispute. In the context of construction disputes in particular, adjudication has proven to be effective in enabling the parties to resolve their disputes in a timely and cost-effective manner (Charrett, 2015).

5.5. Challenging the adjudicator

The most common reason that an adjudicator's decision may be challenged is that he lacks jurisdiction over the matter under dispute (Cook & Kim, 2021). As has been established above, errors of law or fact are not typically grounds for nullifying an adjudicator's decision. In *Carrillion Construction v Devonport Royal Dockyard Ltd* ([2006] BLR 15), Jackson J established 4 key principles in relation to the adjudicator's jurisdiction.

The first is that a decision made by an adjudicator is not the final determination of any of the parties' rights. Secondly, the decision of an adjudicator must be enforced even in the event that it results from an error of law, fact or procedure (*Bouygues UK Ltd v Dahl-Jenson (UK) Ltd* [2004] 1 WLR 2082). Thirdly, if an adjudicator has acted outside of his jurisdiction or in serious breach of the rules of natural justice, a court is not required to enforce the decision (*Balfour Beatty Construction Ltd v The London Borough of Lambeth* [2002] BLR 288). Finally, it is important for judges to pay particular attention to the HGCRA 1996 before they may make a decision as to excessive jurisdiction (*Pegram Shopfitters Ltd v Tally Weijl* [2004] 1 WLR 2082). Furthermore, it is important that the adjudicator's jurisdiction be clearly stipulated in the notice of arbitration.

Following the judgement of *Cantillion Ltd v Urvasco Ltd* ([2008] BLR 250), it is possible to observe that the jurisdiction of the adjudicator may be expanded between the notice and the referral of the dispute. As has been briefly recognised above, the common law identifies two fundamental principles that must be fulfilled in order to achieve a fair procedure. The first is that a person may not be a judge in his own case, and the second is that a person must have the opportunity to have his defence heard. These rules were established in *Copper v Wandsworth Board of Works* ((1863) 14 CB (NS)180). It is widely recognised that, due to the limited timeframe within which the adjudicator must make a decision on a dispute or difference referred to him, there is a potential for him to make an incorrect decision (Barnett, 2016). However, the parties have agreed to the binding nature of the decision, until such time as it is altered by litigation or arbitration. The amendments made to the HGCRA 1996 by the Local Democracy, Economic and Development Act 2009 (LDEDA 2009, s.108(3A)) permit the adjudicator to rectify any mistakes he may have made under the 'slip rule'. It is therefore evident that the rules of adjudication are sufficiently detailed to ensure that the process is fair, and the adjudicator's role is clear. This minimises the potential for parties to challenge the outcome of adjudication in the courts, which undermines the benefits of adjudication in the first place. Thus, the rules surrounding adjudication are designed to preserve this form of ADR, and to only permit judicial intervention in the most serious and deserving of cases in which rules of natural justice have not been followed.

5.6. The technology and construction court and alternative dispute resolution

The construction industry is highly litigious and disputes can be costly, not merely in a financial sense but also in terms of the breakdown of otherwise profitable relationships due to the conflict. While arbitration and adjudication are commonly used in the construction sphere as dispute resolution tools, the adversarial nature of such processes may hold deleterious consequences for parties in terms of financial costs, delays, risks and loss of business. It was not until the late 1980s that it was realised that conventional litigation for construction disputes was far too cumbersome and expensive. Arbitration was the traditional method for the resolution of construction disputes for many years, until the introduction of a range of Alternative Dispute Resolution techniques, adjudication and the introduction of pre-action protocols in litigation. The TCC has also proven eager to embrace ADR during the early stages of litigation proceedings, particularly when litigation costs will exceed the amount in dispute. This section examines the role of the Technology and Construction Court (TCC) in alternative dispute resolution.

5.6.1. The role of the technology and construction court

The TCC is a sub-division of the King's Bench Division, to which disputes involving technology and construction are referred. Since the TCC was formed towards the end of 1998, its reputation has gradually grown, to the extent that it is now regarded as a knowledgeable and capable court (Brooker, 2009: p.88). Accordingly, its case load has significantly increased since 1998 (Constable et al, 2018). The TCC has jurisdiction over construction disputes involving engineering and building, as well as challenges to and the enforcement of adjudication decisions. The TCC's work typically involves complex legal arguments and highly technical issues.

Consequently, TCC judges are required to hear and try some of the most complex and laborious disputes. The TCC adopts a broader definition of Alternative Dispute Resolution (ADR) when compared to traditional definitions. Its definition of ADR is based on "any process that the parties enter into voluntarily" (Shipman, 2006).

The TCC Guide (Courts & Tribunals Service, 2005: para.7.1.1), stipulates that pre-action protocols also involve "formal inter-party negotiations" as an alternative, and states that the protocol is a form "of ADR, because it requires there to be at least one face-to-face meeting between the parties before the commencement of proceedings" (Courts & Tribunals Service, 2005: para.7.2.2).

The TCC is regulated by the Construction and Engineering Court Protocol (Ministry of Justice, 2017), which requires that the parties meet 28 days following the claimant's receipt of the defendant's letter of response (Ministry of Justice, 2017: para.8.2). At the meeting, the parties should consider whether some type of ADR may be deemed "more suitable than litigation", and, if so, they should seek to agree on the form of ADR that will be adopted (Ministry of Justice, 2017: para.12.1).

5.6.2. The TCC's approach to ADR: A case law review

In appropriate cases, the TCC will suggest what form of ADR should be taken, although it generally places the greatest emphasis on mediation in the majority of cases. A rather strict approach is adopted towards parties who refuse to submit their dispute to ADR. *Dunnett v Rail Track Plc* ((2002) CP Rep 35) was the first case in which the Court of Appeal sanctioned a party for its unreasonable refusal to accept an invitation to mediate. However, the judgement did not provide strict guidance on the criteria of unreasonableness to be applied in specific cases. This provoked a number of subsequent cases in which refusals to mediate could be deemed unreasonable (*Reed Solutions plc v Reed Business Information Ltd, Reed Elsevier (UK) Ltd* [2004] EWCA Civ 887; *Paul Gaston, David Boughton v Peter Courtney* [2004] EWHC 600). In *Paul Gaston,* Brooke LJ identified that many cases have great potential to be resolved by a skilled mediator, even those that initially seem to lack promise in terms of being resolved through ADR due to the parties' attitudes.

Such a view was endorsed in *Hurst v Leeming* ([2002] EWHC 1051 (Ch): paras.5-6), in which Lightman J emphasised that:

> *"the mediation process itself can and does often bring about a more sensible and more conciliatory attitude on the parties of the parties than might otherwise be expected to prevail before the mediation" (Also: Multiplex Construction (UK) Ltd v Cleveland Bridge UK Ltd Cleveland Bridge Dorma Long Engineering [2006] EWHC 1341).*

The above principle is representative of the TCC's approach towards ADR in general. The TCC Protocols explicitly state that ADR can result in "significant savings in costs and may result in a settlement which is satisfactory to all parties" (Ministry of Justice, 2017: para.7.1.2). However, there may be some cases in which the costs of ADR may justify the rejection of ADR when it is found to be disproportionately high to the sums involved in the dispute. It has indeed been argued that ADR can be just as costly as litigation, and that considerable costs can arise when settlement is not achieved until close to the court date (Brooker & Lavers, 2005).

Studies imply that ADR is becoming expensive, especially in the event that the parties are familiar with litigation, and intend to use legal representation (Brooker & Lavers, 2005). It has been observed that certain disputes are intrinsically more difficult than others, and that some mediators have greater skills than others (Hill & So, 2010).

This can impact the outcome of the dispute, as well as the ability of the court to determine the extent to which a dispute has a reasonable prospect of success if settled through ADR (*Halsey v Milton Keynes General NHS Trust* [2004] EWCA Civ 576: para.27). It has been argued that a party should not be permitted to use mediation competence or skills (or lack thereof) as a basis for reasonably or unreasonably refusing ADR, because this gives rise to uncertainty in the management and determination of cases (Shipman, 2006). Despite the above claim, mediators' skills have been identified as a key factor that impacts settlement (Bercovitch, 1991). Specialist judges and courts that hear complex construction disputes have been a feature of litigation for a long time.

This has caused parties to construction disputes to seek out expert mediators, with the result that construction mediation is conducted by very few, specialist and expensive mediators. The claim that there is a shortage of construction mediators may suffice to demonstrate that a refusal to mediate is reasonable. However, the existence of the TCC undermines such a conclusion, and renders such a claim unlikely to succeed. This is because the TCC is comprised of judges that offer services in assisting the resolution of a dispute through the most appropriate means.

The TCC has actively participated in guidelines regarding when the parties are required to consider, or may reasonably refuse, ADR. The TCC Protocol requires that the parties consider ADR, however, the

TCC can only exercise discretion to award costs against a successful party in the event that a party claims that the other party's rejection of ADR was unreasonable (Ministry of Justice, 2017: para.4.1).

Case law also reveals the TCC's approach towards ADR for construction disputes. In *Northrup Grumman Mission Systems Europe Ltd v BAE Systems Ltd* ([2014] EWHC 3148 (TCC): para.57), Ramsey J described the case as "like many cases, where points of construction are major issues at the centre of a financial claim". It was emphasised that a mediator could prove effective in bringing the parties together to resolve a dispute that they may not have otherwise proven able to resolve without the assistance of a mediator. In this case, one of the parties had refused to mediate on the basis that it had a strong case. Although Ramsey J agreed that the party did have a strong case, he did not accept that he had reasonably refused to mediate, stating that "mediation had reasonable prospects of success" (para.71). It was upon this basis that the TCC determined that the party had acted unreasonably in refusing to mediate.

A similar approach was adopted by the TCC in *P4 Ltd v Unite Integrated Solutions Plc* ([2006] EWHC 2924 (TCC). Ramsey J focused primarily on the specific features of the case that were considered to render it suitable for mediation or some other form of ADR. For example, the sum under dispute was relatively small, and the parties had a long-term commercial relationship, the preservation of which would have provided both with future benefits (para.45). It was therefore concluded that the refusal to submit the dispute to ADR was unreasonable: "this was a case where I consider that the type of interchanges which mediation or face to face meetings permits, would certainly have stood reasonable prospects of resolving the matter (para.47).

The TCC's favourable approach towards ADR is also reflected in *Ohpen Operations UL Ltd v Invesco Fund Managers Ltd* ([2019] EWHC 2246 (TCC)), in which the TCC stayed the litigation proceedings pending the agreement to mediate. O'Farrell J placed particular emphasis on the fact that "there is a clear and strong policy in favour of enforcing alternative dispute resolution provisions and in encouraging parties to attempt to resolve disputes prior to litigation. (para.58). This demonstrates that the TCC places ultimate focus on the agreement to submit a dispute to ADR, and will not intervene prior to the ADR proceedings, especially where this has been agreed by the parties in the contract.

Once ADR proceedings have actually taken place, but failed to resolve a dispute, the TCC appears to be significantly more sympathetic in its approach. In *Car Giant Ltd & Acredart Ltd v The Mayor and Burgesses of the London Borough of Hammersmith* ([2017] RWHC 464 (TCC)), a party applied to the TCC for an order for indemnity costs following a failed attempt to resolve the dispute through ADR. The party claimed that the other party had unreasonably delayed in agreeing to mediate.

The TCC recognised that mediation or ADR cannot be successful in all cases, regardless of whether it is conducted early or 'late'. It was sufficient that the mediation took place: "any delay in mediating cannot be shown to have caused any increased costs...the courts should be slow to criticise a party's behaviour where decisions such as when to mediate are matters of tactical importance where different views may legitimately be held" (para.27. Also: *Parkway Construction Ltd v Howard De Walden Estates Ltd* ([2014] EWHC 1533 (TCC)). The TCC has also proven able and willing to identify circumstances in which ADR would not have been successful, and have therefore not penalised the parties for the refusal to do so.

This was the case in *Courtwell Properties Ltd v Greencore PF (UK) Ltd* ([2014] EWHC 184 (TCC)), in which the TCC expressed doubt as to whether ADR would have succeeded, hence determining that "the failure to mediate is not a factor to justify the award of indemnity costs" (Akenhead J: para.35. Also: *Imperial Chemical Industries Ltd v Merit Merrell technology Ltd* [2017] EWHC 2299 (TCC), Akenhead J: para.11). Prior to the judgement of Reid Minty v Taylor ([2002] 1 WLR 2800: para.28), it was generally the case that indemnity costs could be awarded for conduct "lacking in moral probity" or "deserving of moral condemnation". In Reid, the court determined that it was no longer necessary to reach such a high standard, meaning that conduct that is "unreasonable to a high degree" is the applicable standard (*Kiam v MGN Ltd (No. 2)* [2002] 1 WLR 2810, Brown LJ: para.12). In *International Ltd & Another v Styrene Packaging and Insulation & Others* ([2005] EWHC 2113 (TCC)), the TCC was required to determine whether the successful party's conduct had reached such a level when he refused to mediate.

The TCC stated that it was not aware of any case in which a refusal to mediate was a "sole justification" for granting indemnity costs, although it did accept that it could be "wholly unjustified to reject an offer to mediate...in exceptional circumstances" (para.9). Ultimately, the TCC denied the claim for indemnity costs on the basis that the successful party had not completely refused mediation. He had in fact agreed to mediate at the time that the offer to mediate was first made, however, the parties could not agree on the form of mediation/ ADR that should be taken. It is evident that the TCC's approach towards ADR is facilitative, but with limits. It does not require that parties to disputes always agree to ADR, due to the realisation that not all construction disputes may be successfully resolved through ADR. Accordingly, the TCC has proven able to adopt a coherent approach towards ADR, based on the specific circumstances of the particular case.

5.7. Summary

This chapter has examined Adjudication, Arbitration and the role of the Technology & Construction Court in the Alternative Dispute Resolution. The case law from the TCC is demonstrative of its facilitative approach towards ADR in general. Indeed, the TCC adopts a rigorous approach towards parties who refuse to submit their dispute to ADR, based on the principle of unreasonableness. The TCC has proven able to impose a coherent concept of reasonableness/unreasonableness in order to distinguish effectively between circumstances in which a party justifiably and unjustifiably refuses to resort to ADR, based on the circumstances of the case.

References

Abwunza, A.A., Peter, T.K. and Muigua, K., (2019). Effectiveness of arbitration in contractual disputes: Tension between procedural efficiency and award quality. Journal of Legal Affairs and Dispute Resolution in Engineering and Construction, 11(2), p.04519003.

Bercovitch, J., (1991). International mediation and dispute settlement: Evaluating the conditions for successful mediation. *Negot*. J., 7, p.17.

Besaiso, H., Fenn, P., & Emsley, M. (2018). Evolution of Construction Arbitration. Journal of Legal Affairs and Dispute Resolution in Engineering and Construction, 10(2).

Brooker, P. and Lavers, A., (2005). Mediation Outcomes: Lawyers' Experience with Commercial and Construction Mediation in the United Kingdom. *Pepp. Disp. Resol. LJ*, 5, p.161.

Brooker, P. and Lavers, A., (2005)a. Construction lawyers' experience with mediation post-CPR. Construction Law Review, 1, pp.19-46.

Constable, A., Garrett, L. and Lamont, C., (2018). *Litigation in the Technology and Construction Court*. Informa Law from Routledge.

Courts & Tribunals Service, (2005). *The Technology and Construction Court Monograph* . (2nd edn.). London: Stationery Office

Charrett, D., (2015). Cost effective resolution of construction disputes. Int'l. In-House Counsel J., 9, p.1.

Cook, R. and Kim, I., (2021). Adjudicator jurisdiction across jurisdictions. CONSTRUCTION LAW INTERNATIONAL, 16(3), p.17.

Ezurmendia, J. and Gonzalez, M.D.L.A., (2021). A comparison between the standard of proof applicable in arbitration and formal adjudication. The International Journal of Evidence & Proof, 25(1), pp.3-15.

Fortese, F. and Hemmi, L., (2015). Procedural fairness and efficiency in international arbitration. Groningen Journal of International Law, 3(1), pp.110-124.

Gould, N. and Linneman, C., (2008). Ten years on: Review of adjudication in the United Kingdom. Journal of Professional Issues in Engineering Education and Practice, 134(3), pp.298-301.

Harmon, K.M., (2003). Resolution of construction disputes: A review of current methodologies. Leadership and Management in Engineering, 3(4), pp.187-201.

Hill, T. and So, D., (2010). Resolving Construction Claims through Mediation. *Asian Disp. Rev.*, 12, p.58.

Housing Grants, Construction and Regeneration Act 1996

Jahren, C.T. and Dammeier, B.F., (1990). Investigation into construction disputes. Journal of Management in Engineering, 6(1), pp.39-46.

Kennedy, P., (2008). Evolution of statutory adjudication as a form of dispute resolution in the UK construction industry. Journal of Professional issues in Engineering Education and practice, 134(2), pp.214-219.

Lee, C.K., Yiu, T.W. and Cheung, S.O., (2016). Selection and use of alternative dispute resolution (ADR) in construction projects—Past and future research. International Journal of Project Management, 34(3), pp.494-507.

Local Democracy, Economic and Development Act 2009

Merrill, T.W., (2018). Fair and Impartial Adjudication. Geo. Mason L. Rev., 26, p.897.

Ministry of Justice, (2017). *Pre-Action Protocol for Construction and Engineering Disputes*. Source: https://www.justice.gov.uk/courts/procedure-rules/civil/protocol/prot_ced.

Scheme for Construction Contracts 1998

Shipman, S., (2006). Court approaches to ADR in the civil justice system. *Civil Justice Quarterly*, 25, pp.181-218.

Case Law

Balfour Beatty Construction Ltd v The London Borough of Lambeth ([2002] EWHC 597 (TCC))

Ballast plc v The Burrell Co (Construction Management) Ltd ([2002] SC 279)

Bouygues UK Ltd v Dahl-Jensen UK Ltd ([2000] BLR 49)

Campbell v Edwards ([1976] 1 WLR 403

Costain Ltd v Strathclyde Builders Ltd ([2004] SLT

Deko Scotland Ltd v Edinburgh Royal Joint Venture & Others [2003] SLT 727

Discain Project Services Ltd. v. Opecprime Development Ltd. ([2001] BLR 285 TCC)

Glencot Development & Design Ltd v Ben Barrett & Son (Contractors) Ltd [2001] EWHC 15 (TCC)).

Macob Civil Engineering Ltd v Morrison Construction Ltd [1999] BLR 93

Nikko Hotels (UK) Ltd v MEPC Plc ([1991] 2 EGLR 103)

Owen Pell Ltd v Bindi (London) Ltd [2008] EWHC 1420 (TCC)

Pegram Shopfitters Ltd v Tally Weijl [2004] 1 WLR 2082

Pepper v Hart ([1993] AC 593

Dunnett v Rail Track Plc (2002) CP Rep 35

Reed Solutions plc v Reed Business Information Ltd, Reed Elsevier (UK) Ltd [2004] EWCA Civ 887

Paul Gaston, David Boughton v Peter Courtney [2004] EWHC 600

Hurst v Leeming [2002] EWHC 1051 (Ch)

Multiplex Construction (UK) Ltd v Cleveland Bridge UK Ltd Cleveland Bridge Dorma Long Engineering [2006] EWHC 1341

Halsey v Milton Keynes General NHS Trust [2004] EWCA Civ 576

Northrup Grumman Mission Systems Europe Ltd v BAE Systems Ltd [2014] EWHC 3148 (TCC)

P4 Ltd v Unite Integrated Solutions Plc [2006] EWHC 2924 (TCC)

Ohpen Operations UL Ltd v Invesco Fund Managers Ltd [2019] EWHC 2246 (TCC)

Car Giant Ltd & Acredart Ltd v The Mayor and Burgesses of the London Borough of Hammersmith ([2017] RWHC 464 (TCC)

Parkway Construction Ltd v Howard De Walden Estates Ltd [2014] EWHC 1533 (TCC)

Courtwell Properties Ltd v Greencore PF (UK) Ltd [2014] EWHC 184 (TCC)

Imperial Chemical Industries Ltd v Merit Merrell technology Ltd [2017] EWHC 2299 (TCC)

Reid Minty v Taylor [2002] 1 WLR 2800

Kiam v MGN Ltd (No. 2) [2002] 1 WLR 2810

International Ltd & Another v Styrene Packaging and Insulation & Others [2005] EWHC 2113 (TCC)

Chapter Six: Dispute Resolution in Construction: An Agenda for Change

6.1 Introduction

Chapter Four traces the perceived need for change recognised over recent years in the construction industry and the need to alter the methods of dispute resolution traditionally used.

6.2. Construction industry

The construction industry has been heavily scrutinised and widely criticised since the mid-1900s, culminating in 1994 with Sir Michael Latham's reports and the consequential implementation of the Housing Grants and Construction Regeneration Act 1996[97]. The major issues highlighted over this period are outlined in this section.

6.2.1. Professional independence

In a contractual situation, it is difficult to imagine how an employer's architect can be impartial and unbiased in matters which may prejudice their employer, much less so in matters which may involve their own professional competence and professional reputation. In 1934, Lord Hansard suggested that: '[t]he principle of the Bill is to prevent parties to contracts from acting as umpires or arbitrators; in fact, to prevent a person being an arbitrator in his own cause'[98]. Yet as recently as 1996, Balfour Beatty[99] entered into an ICE 5th Edition

[97] Simon Report 1944; Banwell Report 1963; Wood Report 1975; Latham Reports: Trust & Money 1993 and Constructing the Team 1994

[98] 2nd Reading, Arbitration Bill, House of Lords, Hansard, Vol 103, 9 Dec 1936

[99] Balfour Beatty Civil Eng v Docklands Light Railway (1996) 78 BLR 42, CA

Standard Form Contract, modified in such a way that the contractor's entitlement was dependent on the employer's judgment with no agreed means of challenging it. The Court emphasised that it was not for it to decide whether the contractor made a good bargain or a bad one, it could only give fair effect to what the parties agreed.

Concerning dispute resolution, this is one example where the industry has failed to change since 1936. Indeed, a key feature identified in Latham's reports (Latham, 1993) was the prevailing lack of independence of the professional architect or engineer in the current marketplace.

6.2.1.1. The Simon and Banwell reports

The first of these reports, the Simon Report (Simon, 1944), examined the placing and management of building contracts. It identified the problem of parties entering into lump-sum building contracts and commencing work on-site before design completion leading to variations from the original contract, often causing delay and extra cost, giving rise to claims for additional payment by the contractor and regularly leading to disputes. The Banwell Report (Banwell, 1964) highlighted that clients seeking an early start continued to be a significant issue in the industry. The report found that such clients are often as unrealistic in the realisation of risks as the contractors who undertake the work.

6.2.1.2. The Wood report

The Wood Report (Wood, 1973) illustrates the persistent nature of the industry's problems. It recommended that contractors should be paid the full cost of pre-priced variations, a practice that has not been embraced by the industry.

The committee recognised the difficulties for construction professionals in maintaining an impartial role and recommended professional bodies consider establishing a procedure for calling in independent experts in cases of dispute and a panel of experts to be called on for prompt decisions on matters of fact in disputes. The suggestion to use independent experts to determine the facts was a step in the direction toward construction adjudication, which the industry has now embraced. In respect of arbitration and the belief that it was expensive and long, the committee disregarded the suggested two-tier system of arbitration. They believed such a 'small claims court' if established for construction would be quickly inundated with work. When we consider the substantial and what appears to be continual growth of adjudication, this may have been sound judgement at the time.

6.2.1.3. The Latham reports

Latham recognised the growing pressure on professionals involved in the construction industry, particularly with the risk of being sued by the client following an unsuccessful contract becoming increasingly common. These professionals believed they were working in a 'watching of backs' (Latham, 1993) culture, making their role in an area where they had to make independent decisions and often decide on their own misdemeanours untenable.

Latham viewed this as a 'call for "independent" adjudication, separate from the traditional professional role of the architect or engineer as contract administrator'(Sheridan, 1993). Latham also perceived a general dissatisfaction with the cost and speed of arbitration as a means of dispute resolution in the construction industry. He alleged there was growing support amongst industry professionals for speedy, independent binding adjudication to be immediately implemented even if challenged after completion. Against this background, Latham produced his final report 'Constructing The Team' in 1994 which served as the impetus for statutory intervention in the UK construction industry. Not only was Latham criticised for the lack of justification to support his belief that compulsory adjudication was the key to settling all disputes in the construction industry (Sheridan, 1993), but Uff (1997) also described him as 'a supporter of the Contractors' lobby and cannot be considered as an "independent and friendly observer" as he claimed in his report. He was certainly a free marketeer and a supporter of the activist state'. Uff (1997) further suggested that Latham's research was flawed and did not reflect the views of the industry at all. Nevertheless, the reports were instrumental in changing the face of dispute resolution in the UK construction industry. These strategic reports highlighted the persistence of many unresolved issues over fifty years in UK construction and whether Latham's statutory adjudication will successfully address these issues remains questionable in the long term.

6.3. Litigation

Dispute resolution is a service industry and must recognise client needs[100]. Indeed, a former Chief Justice of the United States of America, Warren Burger, once said:

> *The obligation of our profession is [...] to serve as healers of human conflict. To fulfil our traditional obligation means that we should provide mechanisms that can produce an acceptable result in the shortest possible time, with the least possible expense and with the minimum of stress on the participants. This is what justice is all about (Coulson, 1984).*

[100] This theme was the cornerstone of Lord Woolf's interim and final reviews of civil litigation, Access to Justice.

Such sentiments have been regularly expressed over many years with respect to the cost and time of the English judicial system before Lord Woolf's reforms. These reforms are significant to the UK construction industry as the majority of construction disputes occur in the English Technology and Construction Court. The English Jurist Jeremy Bentham (1748-1832) considered that the evils of civil process to include expense, vexation, delay and complication (Reynolds, 2000). He blamed lawyers and judges alike for an unfair and inaccessible system.

There was a failed attempt by the Judicature Commissioners in 1877 to reform these 'evils'. However, the constitution of the Courts has been largely untouched until Lord Woolf's Report in 1996 (Woolf, 1996). In recent times the impetus reform of the English civil justice system has continued with the Civil Justice Review (1988) looking at ways of reducing delay, cost and complexity, the Heilborn-Hodge Report (1993) which recommended urgent and radical reform to modernise and improve the civil justice system, and the Woolf Report (1996) which included a draft of new procedural rules which have since been refined.

Lord Woolf found the English civil justice system to be plagued by excessive delay and cost, undue complexity, uncertainty (both as to timetable and cost) and unfairness, particularly where parties were of unequal financial strength.

According to Reynolds, (2000), '[t]he two centuries between the published views of the idealist Bentham and the pragmatist Woolf demonstrate the difficulties surrounding procedural reform and the fact that procedural reform is not achieved easily in the legal system' (Woolf, 1996).

Such reform was not achieved through the introduction of the Civil Procedure Rules by Lord Woolf. However, the procedural difficulties can be appreciated when we consider the concerns expressed in regard to Lord Woolf's drastic increase in the courts' powers of intervention.

6.4. Judicial intervention and innovation

Lord Woolf adopted the concept of case management from the Federal Judicial Council of the United States[101]. However, they have Special Masters to facilitate settlement, avoiding any danger of the judge compromising their position as the independent decision-maker. It is not clear to what extent the English judiciary would be able to encourage settlement and concerns have been raised by many in the academic community that judges may become partially prejudiced as a result of this role and, may in the course of their managerial function as case manager develop a bias to one side or the other[102]. Therefore, Lord Woolf taking the view that the philosophy of litigation should be primarily to encourage early settlement of disputes must be viewed against the spectre of the court persuading parties to accept something less than what they may otherwise be entitled to by law.

As has been said: 'settlements can be fair and prudent arrangements, but can also be squalid scenes of bullying acted out by the law's back alleys'[103] The balance between a completely adversarial process and a limited cost-effective one is difficult to achieve. Is it possible that we are moving toward a more equitable system in terms of accessibility, but also to a more of a pragmatic solution in terms of public justice?

---

[101] See Access to Justice, p.31, para.20. See also criticism of Report in 'Reform of Civil Procedure', Zuckerman and Cranston 1995; 'Why Woolf Reform Should be Rejected', Michael Zander Q.C.

[102] see Rensik: 'Managerial Judges', 96 Harvard Law Review 374 (1982) and Sallman: 'Observations on Judicial Rule Precipitation in Case Load Management' 8 LJQ 129 (1989 at pp139-144)

[103] Andrews, 'Principles of Civil Procedure', para 2-011; similarly, Glasser, 'Civil Procedure and the lawyers-the Advisory Principle and the Decline of Orality Principle' (1993) 56 MLR 307 London School of Economics

This 'need to change' presented primarily by academics and the legal profession has also been recognised by the end-user. Litigation, the legal process and the ways of lawyers and expert witnesses have attracted poor press. For instance, when the law firm Herbert Smith surveyed the 400 largest companies in the UK, the length, complexity and cost of civil justice were widely criticised by respondents.

Indeed, Ian Dixon (Sourdin, 2002) was quoted on one occasion as saying:

> *You can't win if you go to court. The high legal costs are part of it. Litigation is long and repetitive. The legal system is abysmal and inefficient*

It was hoped the implementation of Lord Woolf's reforms would be able to address this commercial perception of an abysmal and inefficient legal system in time. However, these reforms do not extend to the Scottish courts.

6.4.1. Scotland

There is no doubt that the majority of UK construction disputes are decided in the TCC. However, some are heard in the Scottish courts and criticism has also been directed at the commercial system of justice in Scotland. The tide of reviews of civil justice in Scotland from 2009 onwards has provided an impetus to reform of Scottish legal system regarding commercial litigation and consultation on the introduction of mandatory mediation. However, arbitration has gone some way to addressing the inefficiencies of the current system, albeit with some limitations.

6.5. Arbitration

Table 6.1. presents the advantages and disadvantages of arbitration, which has been promoted by its proponents as a no-nonsense method of dispute resolution, relying more on technical assessment than on the application of judicial nuance.

Table 6.1. *Advantages and Disadvantages of Arbitration*

Advantages	Disadvantages
The procedure is flexible rather than subject to set rules and may be tailored to suit the nature of the particular dispute. Short procedures, e.g. arbitration on documents only may be agreed by the parties.	The opportunity to use the High Court summary judgement procedure has been lost where the parties have an arbitration agreement, with the loss of the court's discretion whether to grant a stay of proceedings.
It is private and confidential.	Disadvantages with confidentiality, particularly when disclosure of arbitration documents to a third party is of positive benefit to a party to an arbitration agreement.
The tribunal may be chosen by the parties. Arbitrators with appropriate technical expertise may be selected.	Arbitrators charge substantial fees, often including fees which are not earned but are difficult to avoid, in the form of minimum and commitment fees.
It is less formal than litigation.	There is often scope for jurisdiction arguments in arbitration, giving rise to additional costs.
There is more scope for representation other than by solicitors or counsel.	While the procedure is flexible, it is also uncertain. In court proceedings, for example there are defined rules about disclosure of documents. In arbitration, the rules have to be devised for each arbitration and this carries a cost.
In International arbitration, the New York Convention provides for effective enforcement throughout the commercial world.	Some remedies are available only in court proceedings, e.g. injunctions.
	Arbitrators tend in general to have a laxer approach to procedural matters such as the particularity of pleadings, which can make arbitral procedures less effective than court proceedings.

	The difficulty in joining parties to arbitrations and in consolidating separate arbitration proceedings is a major problem, given the number of parties involved in construction and engineering projects. This facto alone, coupled with the removal of the courts discretion to refuse a stay on the basis that there is a multi-party dispute, may well be sufficient to persuade employers to avoid arbitration agreements. Arbitrators often appear not to be fearless, in the sense that they have a concern about the appearance of bias. Judges do not hesitate to decide cases entirely against one party, if it is how they assess the merits. Arbitrators seem much more likely to decide that one party should succeed in some respects, the other party in other respects.

However, many commentators regard it as rather legalistic and Sir John Donaldson MR stated: 'arbitration is usually no more and no less than litigation in the private sector'[104]. Similar concerns have been expressed in Australia:

> *'Arbitration has broken down as a cheap and efficient means of resolving construction disputes, albeit that the cause may be the strenuously adversarial manner in which the disputants themselves pursue the arbitral process' (NPWC/NBCC,1990).*

[104] Northern Regional Health Authority v Derek Crouch Construction Company Ltd [1984] 1 QB 644

6.5.1. Limitations of arbitration

According to many industry commentators, arbitration in the construction industry has failed to live up to its promise and in many instances has proved more inflexible than litigation. It is unsuitable where questions of law are significant or for multi-party disputes where not all the parties are bound by arbitration; a common phenomenon in the construction industry involving disputes with complex loss and expense claims, poor workmanship or design and often involving several parties (Gould et al, 1999).

The lawyers have led arbitration to mirror a High Court hearing rather than a procedure decided by the parties and the benefits of speed and flexibility have disappeared and arbitrators are reluctant to take a more active role in managing cases to minimise this tendency for fear of allegations of misconduct. There are particular areas in the construction industry where extensive time and costs are an inevitable result of dispute resolution. Such costs would be lower in litigation where the judge and court facilities are provided at public expense, in contrast to arbitration where the parties must bear the cost of the arbitrator and facilities themselves.

Privacy is often promoted as an advantage of arbitration over litigation. However, it has been said that 'construction disputes rarely excite the blood of the popular press (Diggle & Hogan 1997), implying privacy advantages of arbitration may be more apparent than real. Indeed, this confidentiality may in itself create problems for a party wishing to make use of materials, which came to light in the arbitration, at any subsequent litigation.

The Arbitration Act 1996 was considered necessary because the arbitration law as it stood was diffuse and unclear in some important respects, including the extent of the arbiter's immunity for negligence;

and it failed to support the arbitrator and clarify their authority, leading to delaying tactics, excessive cost and complexity in what was supposed to be a simplified means of dispute resolution.

6.5.2. Arbitration Act 1996

In 1989, the Mutsill Committee recommended the development of a new Arbitration Act. This initiative was developed in several key stages, involving a drafting bid prepared under the Marriot Working Group and then under the umbrella of the Department of Trade and Industry. Following a much-criticised draft bill, published in 1994, Lord Saville became the chairman of the Department Advisory Committee (DAC) which published a new draft paper in 1995. The Arbitration Act received royal assent in June 1996.

6.5.3. Review of the Arbitration Act 1996

The Law Commission has recently announced a review of the Arbitration Act 1996 some 25 years after the legislation first came into force. The review aimed to 'enhance the experience for those who choose to arbitrate in England and Wales and maintain English law as the gold standard in international arbitrations.

Those consulted about the review hope that it will provide an opportunity to ensure that the Act reflects modern arbitration practices more generally. At the time the Act came into force 25 years ago, it represented a ground-breaking attempt to draw together the fragmented legislation and case law governing arbitration as it then stood in England and Wales.

The review of the 1996 Act follows reviews and reforms of equivalent legislation in other jurisdictions including the introduction of the International Arbitration (Amendment) Act 2020 which amended the Singapore International Arbitration Act and the ongoing review of the Arbitration Law of the People's Republic of China. Although the scope of the review of the 1996 Act is still to be finalised, the Law Commission has identified possible areas for reform, which include:

- the power to summarily dismiss meritless claims or defences in arbitration proceedings;
- the courts' powers exercisable in support of arbitration proceedings;
- the procedure for challenging a jurisdiction award;
- the availability of appeals on points of law;
- the law concerning confidentiality and privacy in arbitration proceedings; and
- electronic service of documents, electronic arbitration awards and virtual hearings.

Reform in these areas, if implemented, should assist in managing the costs of London-seated arbitrations and clarifying the parties' obligations relating to important matters such as confidentiality, which is not currently expressly dealt with in the 1996 Act.

The Act deliberately made no express provision for arbitration proceedings to be confidential unlike in other jurisdictions such as Australia which has an opt-out system. Instead, confidentiality is implied at common law, albeit the limits of that obligation '*are still in the process of development on a case-by-case basis*' (see the Court of Appeal case of *John Forster Emmott v Michael Wilson & Partners Limited*).

This inherent *flexibility* that the Courts have in interpreting the Act (or gaps left by the Act) is regarded by some as a strength and others as a weakness, albeit familiarity with the Act and how it works in practice has historically been cited as a reason for not amending the Act significantly if at all. In a leading speech in 2016, Lord Thomas (then Lord Chief Justice of England and Wales) argued that:

'In retrospect the UK went too far in 1979 and again in 1996 in favouring the perceived advantages for arbitration as a means of dispute resolution in London over the development of the common law; the time is right to look again at the balance. There is also a need to examine whether other markets would be prepared to follow the financial markets, to waive arbitration in cases where there were significant points of general interest and to appreciate that not only would their own dispute, in the right case involving legal issues, be better determined in a court but, more importantly, the wider interests of their industry and of the common law in general would be much better served by more issues being resolved in court and the law thus developed and clarified'.

The effect of arbitration (and the lack of case law) can, for example, be seen in relation to standard form construction contracts such as FIDIC which provide for arbitration as their default final dispute resolution mechanism. This is unhelpful when it comes to interpreting such contracts compared to forms such as the JCT where a wealth of case law exists. The Law Commission is currently in the pre-consultation phase of the reform process. Nevertheless, the Commission has made it clear that the overwhelming response from the arbitration community is that the Act works well and that "root and branch reform" is not desired.

6.5.4. The statutory framework for arbitration in Scotland

In contrast to other jurisdictions including England, the Scots law of arbitration was based almost entirely on the common law developed over several hundred years, since the 25th Act of the Articles of Regulations 1695. This has occurred mainly by reference to the contractual nature of proceedings and has been only marginally affected by statute[105]. According to Dundas:

---

[105] Scottish Government (2008) Consultation on Arbitration (Scotland) Bill, ISBN 978-0-7559-5791

> *'The lack of a codifying statute setting out a modern comprehensive Scots law on arbitration has been the subject of much controversy and has been stated as the principal reason for the decline of commercial arbitration in Scotland in recent years' (Dundas, 2010).*

At this point, the then Scottish Government established a committee to 'review and recommend changes to provide a modern and effective arbitration framework in Scotland'. The Dervaird Committee produced a report and draft Arbitration Bill which has since been updated (Dundas, 2010). However, the new legislation was never introduced due to a lack of parliamentary time. According to Mather (2010) this is 'now a devolved matter and any legislation had to be enacted by the Scottish Parliament'. He further suggested that 'the deficiencies in the current law of arbitration including the absence of a common-law power to award damages or to award interest before the date of decree arbitral have had to be addressed by practical means' (Mather, 2010).

According to Scott (2010):

> *'Arbiters have to be given such power by the parties (a) in the arbitration clause itself, (b) in the Deed of Appointment or Submission or (c) by adopting a set of Rules such as The Scottish Arbitration Code promulgated by the Scottish Council for International Arbitration, Scottish Building Contracts Commission and the Chartered Institute of Arbitrators (Scottish Branch).'*

These rules do not just establish procedural rules for the conduct of arbitrations and as Scott has explained 'they alter the legal rights and obligations of parties and their terms should be considered carefully before adopting Rules in whole or in part'.

6.5.5. The Arbitration (Scotland) Act 2010

As has been seen, arbitration law in Scotland was derived primarily from case law, rather than being codified. Accordingly, the position was not readily clear or accessible with gaps and difficulties in establishing the actual nature of the law.

This is in contrast to many other jurisdictions where clear statutory frameworks are in place. Although Scotland did have some Rules or Codes regarding arbitration sponsored by interested organisations, these were without statutory backing and thus did not have adequate force. The Scottish courts have supported arbitration, but their role was not altogether clear (Shaw, 2010). In the absence of a clear statutory framework, arbitration can prove more time-consuming and expensive than it need be. These issues resulted in calls for an easily accessible and clear statutory framework to be incorporated into the law of Scotland. After a draft Bill and consultation process, on 30th January 2009 the Arbitration (Scotland) Bill was published by the Scottish Government. The Arbitration (Scotland) Act 2010 (the 'Scottish Act') received Royal Assent on 5th January 2010 and came into force on 7th June 2010. The Arbitration (Scotland) Act 2010 modernized and codified the law in statute to bring it into line with up to date arbitral practices in other jurisdictions. The Scottish Government hopes that the Act will lead to a revival of arbitration as a method of resolving construction disputes.

6.6. Summary

This chapter has identified the widespread dissatisfaction with the traditional forms of dispute resolution available in the construction industry. The sheer complexity of construction disputes often leading to expensive, time-consuming and stressful paths being trodden through the traditional resolution procedures made it clear that, wherever possible, an alternative approach was required in this adversarial industry. In many instances, the issues raised in disputes are not clearly delineated and do not lend themselves to either litigation or arbitration, a fact which is all too often ignored or recognised only after proceedings have commenced. This can lead to the adverse effects of:

- polarised positions;
- a drain on a client's managerial time;
- clients who feel out of touch with their own dispute and the victims of a legal take-over;
- damaged commercial relationships;
- expensive and long-drawn-out proceedings;
- use of deliberate delaying tactics by a defendant who knows how to play the system;
- a pyrrhic victory for the successful litigant with monies recovered representing a mere fraction of actual expenditure;
- a judgment that is impossible to enforce;
- a belated realisation by the plaintiff that the principal reason for the litigation or arbitration was the impecuniosity of the defendant; and
- lawyers who are reluctant to engage in early reality-testing with their client.

Therefore, the need for the development of new dispute resolution techniques in the construction industry has taken on some urgency since the 1980s with the importation of ADR from the US. Although, it has been demonstrated that negotiation allows the greatest party control and litigation/arbitration the least, the perceived failure of litigation and arbitration may to lead to a substantial growth of ADR in UK construction. This aspect is discussed a greater length in chapter six.

References

Banwell, Sir Harold. (1964) The Placing and Management of Contracts for Building and Civil Engineering Work, HMSO, London.

Bok, D (1983) A Flawed System of Law Practice and Training, Journal of Legal Education, 570, p 570-571

Coulson, R (1984) Professional Mediation of Civil Disputes, American Arbitration Association, p. 6-7

Diggle, M, & Hogan, A (1997) Construction Disputes and the Arbitration Act 1996, Construction Law Journal, Volume 13 (6), Sweet & Maxwell.

Dundas, H (2010) The Arbitration (Scotland) Act 2010: Converting Vision into Reality, Arbitration, 76, p 2-15

Gould, N, Capper, P, Dixon, G and Cohen, M (1999) Dispute resolution in the construction industry, 1st Edition, Thomas Telford, ISBN 0727728369.

NPWC/NBCC (1990) No dispute: strategies for improvement in the Australian building and construction industry. Report by NPWC/NBCC Joint Working Party.

Latham, M. (1993) Trust and Money, Interim report of the Joint Government/ Industry Review of Procurement and Contractual arrangements in the United Kingdom Construction Industry, HMSO, London

Mather, J (2010) Forum of choice? The journal online: the members' magazine of the law society of Scotland, 15 February

Reynolds, M (2000) Construction Litigation Practice, Sweet & Maxwell, London, p143

Scottish Consumer Council (2005). The Civil Justice System in Scotland–A Case for Review (2005: Edinburgh) Sheriff Court Phase 2. Scottish Executive Central Research Unit.

Scott, D (2010) New Arbitration Act for Scotland, January 21

Simon, Sir Ernest (1944) The Placing and Management of Contracts, HMSO, London

Shaw, M (2010) The Arbitration Act - A New Beginning in Scotland? 12 January.

Sheridan, P (1999) Construction and Engineering Arbitration, Sweet & Maxwell, ISBN: 9780421589209, p508.

Sourdin, T (2002) Alternative Dispute Resolution, Lawbook Company, ISBN 0 455 21820 X

Wood, Sir Kenneth (1975) The Public Client and the Construction Industries, Building and Civil Engineering Economic Development Councils chaired by Sir Kenneth Wood, HMSO, London

Lord Woolf (1996) Access to Justice (Report to Lord Chancellor on the civil justice system in England and Wales), July.

Uff, J (1997) Construction contract reform: A plea for sanity, Construction Law Press, London

Chapter Seven: The Construction Industry and Alternative Dispute Resolution

7.1 Introduction

The former Dean of Harvard Law School, Derek Bok, in a discussion regarding the shortcomings of the litigation process said:

> *Most people find their legal rights severely compromised by the cost of legal services, the baffling complications of existing rules and procedures and the long, frustrating delays involved in bringing proceedings to a conclusion. From afar, therefore, the legal system looks grossly inequitable and inefficient (Bok,1983, 571)*

It is this kind of sentiment that has justified and encouraged the establishment and growth of alternative methods of dispute resolution in many areas of the world, particularly the USA[106]. This chapter provides an overview of the main options available an assessment of their strengths and weaknesses individually, and in comparison, with arbitration and litigation.

7.2. Outside influences

The UK can no longer plough its own furrow regarding methodology to address dispute resolution particularly as multi-national business interests need and want consistent approaches to their contract arrangements in their various markets. While laws will always have regional variations, ADR and in particular consensual ADR

---

[106] Japan, Dispute Resolution and Conflict Management in Construction – An International Review, Fenn, O'Shea and Davies

can operate in a similar manner irrespective of geography. Binding solutions can also be obtained via the UNCITRAL Model Law 1985 for arbitration of international disputes.

Settling disputes using ADR procedures places control primarily in the hands of the parties who can reach a settlement that suits their business needs and requirements. Prosecution of their relative rights and obligations under law may not necessarily be in their best interests. It also has a track record throughout the business world of being slow, demanding of senior management time and expensive with funds flowing out of the business to legal advisors. Governments and major business interests have similar objectives in this area; to reduce the time involved in getting to settlement and to reduce the cost of disputes. The result has been a global growth in the use of alternative methods of dispute resolution.

Japanese companies and their contacts have traditionally been averse to conflict and they employ "good-faith negotiation" clauses in contracts whereby the parties will settle differences amicably[107]. Disputes are settled by "saiban gai no wakai" and the common form of consensual resolution is "chotei". Japan through its preferred practice of avoiding confrontation in commercial arrangements has provided a paradigm of how commercial arrangements could be conducted without, or at worst with minimal, conflict.

The United States took the lead in development of alternative procedures with the US Army Corp of Engineers among others setting up dispute review boards and developing forms of partnering contracts from the 1980's onwards. These actions were taken to reduce conflict and to manage it more effectively when it arose. Case

[107] Public Law 105-315 codified at 28 USC, ss. 651 et seq

management and ADR was trialed in various districts of California around the same time and the 1990 Civil Justice Reform Act formalised the use of ADR in the court system.

This reform was given further impetus by the Alternative Disputes Resolution Act of 1998 that allowed ADR to be used in all civil cases, ADR had to be considered by all civil litigants and the court could compel parties to try ADR. This provides obvious parallels with Rule 26.4 of the new Civil Procedure Rules. It also requires the federal district courts to set up ADR programmes and to provide support for its use.

The United States have initially through public bodies like the US Army Corp and the Federal Courts developed strategies that addressed the issue of too many disputes taking too long to resolve at significant cost to all parties including the public purse. Various trials and studies by the RAND Corporation and others proved satisfactorily the worth of these alternative methods and legislation brought ADR into the national, and from there the international, forum.

Many other nations quickly grasped the knowledge and experience evolved in these early trial projects and developed their own ADR solutions for settling disputes. Australia, Canada, South-East Asia and many parts of the European Union (EU) now employ ADR as part of their statutory framework for dispute disposal. Experience of international good practice in contract relations and dispute management has and will inevitably continue to affect the UK's way and, as a result Scotland's way, of dealing with commercial disputes. The experience will act as a significant prop to the Government's own actions.

This type of system development is apparent in the move in the UK towards "partnering" forms of contract that only a few years ago were alien to commercial arrangements in this country. Partnering particularly in large public works contracts has been a common method of procurement in the USA and Australia since the early 1990's and Government policy started to move the same way in the UK in the late 1990's. Partnering is a key method of controlling conflict, the consensual ADR techniques can be applied in these types of arrangement to settle disputes, if they arise, and so moves into the partnering forms of contract will reinforce the employment of ADR procedures in contract administration.

7.3. Conflict management

The construction industry has become increasingly aware of the substantial legal costs it burdens itself with as a consequence of its high incidence of disputes.

This expenditure, which globally represents a substantial sum each year, is by no means reflective of the hidden costs of disputes, such as the damage to reputations and commercial relationships, the cost of time spent by executive personnel and the cost of lost opportunities. Campbell (1997) has suggested construction professionals have a responsibility to society to reduce construction risks, one such risk being expensive dispute resolution proceedings and their associated costs. One approach to reducing the incidence of risk (dispute resolution mechanisms), was presented in 1998 by Astor and Chinkin (1998) as:

> *'The need for ongoing dispute resolution mechanisms which are established at the time the contract is entered into, or shortly afterwards. This has been especially the case in the construction industry, where the long-term nature and complexity of many projects and the claim-prone nature of the industry means that a variety of both large and small claims can be anticipated throughout the contract performance. What is often desired is a means of resolving these disputes with a minimum of delay and*

while allowing performance to continue. Where decision-maker(s) can also build up familiarity with the contract and its performance, the mechanism is likely to be more effective' (Astor & Chinkin, 1998, 147).

Competitive forces in the construction industry continue to increase with more contractors chasing fewer contracts leading to reduced profit margins and the assumption of greater risk. The construction industry of today has adopted several techniques such as dispute review boards (DRBs) and partnering to manage these risks and address conflict as it arises in construction projects.

7.3.1. Dispute review boards (DRBs)

A DRB is established at the beginning of the project and normally consists of three members, either one senior executive from each contractual party and a neutral[108] or three independent experts[109]. On very large multi-discipline, multi-contract projects, a pool of experts may be drawn from to deal with disputes as they develop[110], whereas on smaller projects a DRB may only consist of only one expert. With regular DRB visits to site allowing frequent claim review meetings and active involvement of the board throughout construction, it becomes part of the project allowing it to keep abreast of project developments and provide a speedy decision or recommendation on a dispute when required.

The jurisdiction and mode of operation of the board is defined by the parties to the contract. The decisions of the board may be non-binding,

---

[108] Earliest reported use was Boundary Dam in Washington in the 1960s.

[109] Australia, Quebec

[110] Canada, Switzerland, USA

binding unless notice to arbitrate or litigate is given in a specified period[111], or fully and immediately binding.

One of the perceived disadvantages of an immediately binding decision is the 'win-lose' situation which leads to parties developing attitudes, engaging counsel and formalising adversarial approaches to win the action, often leading to damaged working relationships. A decision that is not automatically binding can produce useful information or observations covering both equity and law and assist the parties in negotiating a fair and just settlement, thereby preserving relationships. Unlike other forms of ADR such as mediation or conciliation, DRBs are often not 'without prejudice' therefore processes and their decisions are admissible in later proceedings. One can envisage the influence such a decision by three experienced and impartial construction experts highly familiar with the project may have on a future arbitrator or judge. It is therefore not surprising that most parties appear willing to accept these decisions as the final determination of the dispute. Under the appropriate contractual arrangements, this form of dispute resolution is similar to statutory adjudication, particularly where a DRB decision is binding pending final resolution by arbitration or litigation which is often excluded until substantial completion of the contract. However, the advantages of a DRB that is familiar with the ongoing development and progress of a project, unlike the adjudicator who becomes involved only at the point of dispute, cannot be underestimated particularly in large-scale construction projects.

In the US, Dispute Boards have been employed on projects for many years and studies undertaken by the Florida Highways Authority show that 97% of disputes referred to a board settled before litigation. Genton (2002) agrees by observing that because the parties are paying

---

[111] See Channel Tunnel Group v Balfour Beatty Const. [1993] AC 334

for the board anyway, they are more inclined to use it for advice on potential disputes. Given the high level of disputes which arise in the UK Construction Industry and the fact that dispute boards have been popular in the US for several years, one might question why they have been little used in the UK.

A 2008 survey found that there are still many barriers to be overcome by Dispute Boards if they are to play a more significant role in UK construction (Bowes, 2008). The major barriers appear to be connected with a lack of knowledge and understanding of clients and an unwillingness to pay for something that may or may not be required, particularly on anything other than large projects. The well-documented success of DBs in other countries, particularly the US, shows that they can be a useful form of dispute avoidance and resolution. The use of DBs on the London 2012 Olympic projects alongside a separate adjudication panel could help to improve practitioners' knowledge and promote their use elsewhere in the UK. The provision for dispute boards is no longer the preserve of the FIDIC forms of contract and other contract forms have now followed suit.

Internationally, DRBs are replacing traditional resolution techniques and with the World Bank and FIDIC arrangements, DRBs have replaced the engineer as the first tier of dispute resolution. The DRB does not have the conflict of simultaneously being project designer, employer's agent and adjudicator of disputes and so impartiality has been restored. The NEC now includes an additional dispute resolution clause in its NEC4 contracts providing for the use of a dispute avoidance board (Option W3), albeit it advises that this is not suitable for use in the UK, and the JCT has now issued its 2021 dispute adjudication board document.

The cost of a DRB has been estimated at 0.1%-0.3% of the project cost (Campbell, 1997), which is significant on smaller projects and undoubtedly easier to justify on larger ones. However, compared to litigation or arbitration costs, it is a cost-effective option. Its success can be measured by the fact that very few DRB decisions have been referred to either arbitration or court. This however can also be said about statutory adjudication in the UK construction industry[112]. It is a more cost-effective process for smaller projects whereby they would not be carrying process costs for dispute resolution they may never use.

7.3.2. Partnering

Partnering or alliancing involves the collaboration of major organisations (i.e. client, contractor and design consultants) early in the project to establish communication, forge partnerships and set common goals in the hope of avoiding disputes Bennet & Jayes, 1995). Partnering can be described as an attitude in which mutual trust and project goals have priority over individual agendas. The process is established to manage disputes that may occur during the construction process and can be either binding or non-binding.

It does not necessarily alter the legal and contractual relationship between the parties and may simply shift the focus of responsibility for solving problems from the individual to the team (Barlow et al, 1997). It is important for any firm or group of firms deciding to operate under partnering principles to appreciate that an attitude of mutual trust will only work as a top-down process. This is crucial to ensuring that on-site personnel do not inhibit the resolution of problems due to a misplaced belief that they must hold out for the best possible deal.
Partnering in the UK Construction Industry (Bennet & Jayes, 1998) has been an area of considerable interest in the UK in recent years (Eubanks

---

[112] Only 2% decisions being challenged – see Draper, M (2002) Adjudication down at the crossroads, Construction Law, Volume 13 (9), p14-17.

& Bruno, 1995). Bennett and Jayes (1998) illustrate how to create win-win relationships which involve a sophisticated strategy and require a willingness to improve joint performance. They cite remarkable potential savings of 40–50% in both cost and time. Similarly, Barrick (1998) identifies instances of comparable success. Groups such as Esso, Sainsbury's and the British Airports Authority (BAA) are reported to have reached savings of 40% on costs and 70% on time.

Other research is similarly optimistic in claiming that there is a desire to move beyond narrow self-interest toward a spirit of cooperation and trust (Wood and McDermott, 1999) and that partnering can indeed lead to benefits for all parties (Hamza, 2002)

Lamont (2001) even suggests that people feel genuinely empowered as a direct result of partnering and thereby work together more effectively. Bresnen and Marshall (2002) observe that the literature is replete with case study examples of successful partnerships. However, there is less critical analysis of sufficient empirical depth examining the nature of partnering in practice and whether the claims made for it are consistently justified. Much of the partnering literature tends to concentrate on success stories which are largely anecdotal and focus on the experiences of exemplar organisations. Following the recession that was prevalent through the late 2000's and into the early 2010's it was reported by Hughes et al (2012) that, due to the economic crisis, partnering saw diminishing support.

This could have been the result of clients resorting to the traditional relationships that they were familiar and comfortable with, or it could have been the result of organisations either not having the resources to invest in the development of the process or that they were unwilling to invest the resources during the period of economic uncertainty.

7.3.3. Collaboration, early involvement and dispute avoidance

Since the publication of the Latham Report (1994) and the Egan Report (1996) collaborative working relationships have been in and out of vogue in the construction industry. In the period 2000 to 2005 there was a marked increase in the implementation of information and communication technologies (ICT) (Shelbourne et al, 2007). The introduction of ICT enabled collaborative working to form part of the construction industry's everyday practices. Collaboration was established as being key to improving the industry in the Latham Report. However, through the recession that began around 2007 the industry resorted to "jungle warfare" with suicidal tendering practices (Gardner, 2014). Very quickly after the start of the recession, many organisations reverted back to their previous practices, setting aside all that they had learnt after from the Latham Report.

There is an increasing commitment in the UK construction industry to implement and operate a collaborative process. The existing forms of contract have been amended over time to take cognisance of this desire to increase collaborative working. These changes have been driven by a reluctance within the industry to move away from systems that they are familiar with. There have been numerous initiatives in the UK to minimise the perceived adversarial nature of the industry. For example, the UK Government's Construction Playbook emphasises the benefits of long-term strategic, collaborative contractual relationships and endorses the RICS Conflict Avoidance Pledge which supports collaborative working, use of early intervention techniques when disputes arise and early resolution of potential disputes.

The Construction Avoidance Pledge are all part of a movement, which is also reflected in the standard form contracts, with both NEC4 and FIDIC 2017 embracing language that emphasises avoidance.

Recent comments from the chair of the working party tasked with promoting the RICS-inspired Conflict Avoidance Protocol are indicative of the increased appetite for early intervention techniques in the UK construction industry.

> *'The UK, Scottish and Welsh Governments are very much looking for the construction industry to adopt a much more collaborative approach to procurement and construction [...] This Conflict Avoidance Process fits in very neatly there because it allows people that are seeing issues developing in contracts to sit down with a third party and work with them to get these issues resolved so that they don't escalate into full blown disputes, which are rife in the industry and cost an absolute fortune, and causing all sorts of relationship problems'.*

Institutions and employers (including RICS) launched the voluntary conflict avoidance pledge to reduce the costs of disputes, deliver major projects on time and budget and to promote conflict avoidance techniques. RICS, in conjunction with Transport for London, created the conflict avoidance panel (CAP) process, which has been included in some Transport for London project contracts. The CAP creates a collaborative culture and early intervention is used to deal with disputes. The panel gives impartial information and guidance to all parties to help them resolve differences without court, arbitration or adjudication proceedings.

There is an increasing commitment in the construction industry to implement and operate a collaborative process. The existing forms of contract have been amended over time to take cognisance of this desire to increase collaborative working. These changes have been driven by a reluctance within the industry to move away from systems that they are familiar with.

Figure 7.1 illustrates a raft of modern management concepts all of which can contribute to creating an environment which is likely to be non-adversarial and which may assist in the avoidance of disputes. Many of these concepts that encompass the roles of stakeholders and the alignment of organisational and individual goals.

Figure 7.1. *Pareto influence curve with management concepts superimposed (after McGeorge and Palmer)*

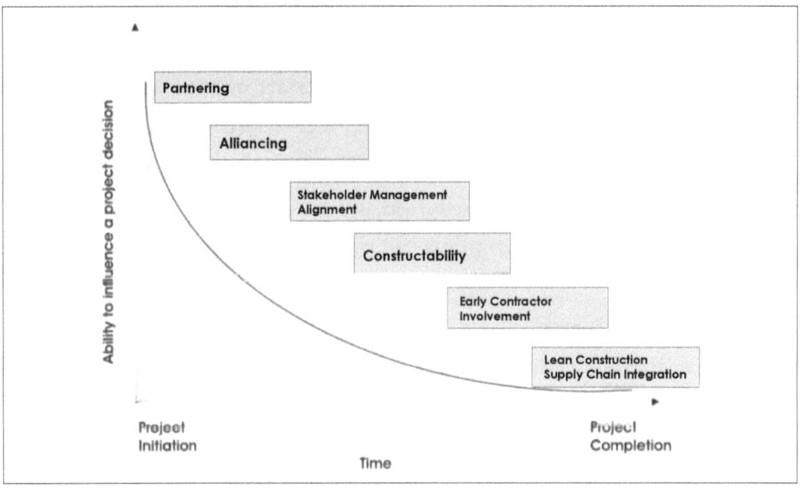

McGeorge and Palmer (2002) state that:

> *'The probability is that the relatively slow and patchy uptake of modern construction management concepts is due not so much to the lack of diligence or a reluctance on the part of construction industry practitioners to adopt new ideas, but to the fact that these concepts need firstly to be understood and studied in total. Secondly, although government agencies are encouraging and, in some cases attempting to enforce the adoption of the concepts, no advice is being given on how these concepts can be applied concurrently and in combination. What is need is a weltanschauung or 'world view' based on a solid knowledge of the individual concepts.'*

Figure 7.1. is illustrative of a range of concepts which may produce a non-adversarial culture and hence avoid disputes. Although there is an inherent risk in attempting to link the concepts through a single theme, there is obvious evidence of systems thinking in a number, if not all, of the concepts, with emphasis on a holistic approach. McGeorge and Palmer (2002), argue that systems thinking carries with it an undercurrent of stakeholder involvement which is clearly evident in concepts such as alliancing and partnering.

The work by Shelbourn et al (*2007*) established that one of the reasons for the uptake of collaborative business relationships organisations to working collaboratively was the lack of a form of contract that embraced the new ways of working. This is supported by the paper produced by Hawkins (2013) where he reports having encountered complaints of contracts not allowing parties to collaborate.

From the literature it is unclear whether this tendency towards utilising a formal contract to support a collaborative relationship stems from the traditional contracting practices in the construction industry and the reliance of organisations on systems that they are familiar with. Hawkins (2013) also suggests that there is a general trend to contract for failure, putting in place conditions that protect the position of organisations in the event that something goes wrong, suggesting that many traditional contracts are developed without the parties actually identifying what is crucial to them.

Wamuziri and Seywright (2005) suggest that, to achieve true collaboration, a legally binding contract that is aligned to the motivations of the parties is essential, concluding that an optimal contract would be an incentive contract, such as a target cost contract. By implementing a formal contract structure, organisations can make use of methods which incentivise the parties to improve performance such as the introduction of a target cost contract. Such a pricing mechanism promotes cost savings while distributing the savings proportionately between the parties, engendering a win-win culture that is important within a collaborative relationship.

7.3.4. The pitfalls of partnering and collaborative business relationships

The framework for collaborative working relationships sets out a relatively simple, easy to follow process which has been constructed with a view of being suitable for organisations no matter what size they are. Why then, if they provide all the benefits that they are reported to do, are all organisations not falling over themselves to implement collaborative working relationships?

While trying to answer this question, it has become apparent from the information available and studies carried out that collaboration is increasing in popularity and it is difficult to find any adversarial reports on collaborative working relationships. Many of the large construction companies are all positively promoting collaboration and are using their willingness to collaborate as a selling point for their organisation. In a study undertaken by Brensen and Marshall (2005) it is highlighted that the construction industry is historically fragmented and it is suggested that it is this fragmentation of the industry that makes implementing collaborative relationships more difficult as, in order to overcome this, it is often necessary to change people's attitudes towards the relationship.

In a further study carried out by Brensen and Marshall (2005) it is established that partnering not only requires a set of practices or techniques to be formed but also requires attitudes and behaviours to be altered to enable the implementation of the principles to be a success.

In this study, Brensen and Marshall investigate whether the co-operation required of a collaborative working relationship is something that should be engineered or if it can be equally as successful if it evolves from previous relationships. The conclusion of this study is that success of a collaborative relationship is not merely a case of applying certain tools and techniques rather it is the result of a complex and dynamic process whereby informal processes are just as important as formal mechanisms. In his article, Taylor (2012) highlights that there is a difference between wanting to work collaboratively and actually committing to working collaboratively, suggesting that the success of a collaborative business relationship is very much centred around the organisation's culture and their willingness to work in the true spirit of collaboration. Taylor goes on to suggest that the success of collaborative working has to be supported from the management of the organisation.

From the literature review undertaken, it is apparent that there has been, and that there continues to be, great discussion over what the term collaboration actually means. There are a number of iterations of contractual relationships which can be considered to be collaborative working relationships. These include joint ventures, alliancing, partnering, teamwork and coalition (Xiaolong et al, 2010) - where the parties were encouraged to form better relationships, working together as opposed to against each other to achieve their objectives. There is a mixed message from the studies undertaken into the success of the collaborative working relationships.

7.4. Alternative dispute resolution: A continuum

Despite litigation and arbitration's ability to produce a final and binding decision, the construction industry has sought the establishment of informal processes for the quick and effective resolution of disputes. ADR is providing various possibilities in place of costly and time-consuming litigation. ADR is broadly defined as 'any method by which conflicts and disputes are resolved privately and other than through litigation in the public courts'[113]. It can include both binding and non-binding procedures. A sliding scale of ADR techniques has evolved over the years including a progression from self-deterministic to third part methods including negotiation, mediation, conciliation, neutral evaluation, expert determination, adjudication and arbitration (Cheeks, 2003).

Figure 7.2 illustrates a continuum of dispute resolution procedures with control of the outcome compared to an assumed escalating degree of resolution costs and hostilities.

Figure 7.2: *Dispute Resolution Continuum*

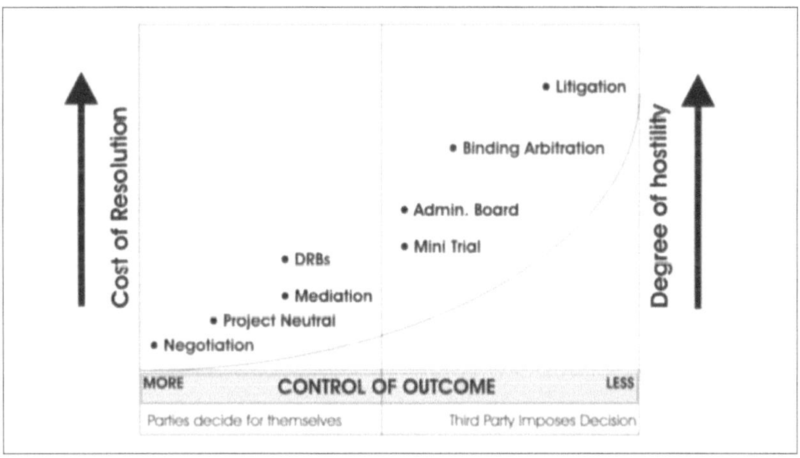

The shift in focus toward processes outside the courts is mainly due to the adversarial nature of the litigation process. It is a process which has long been identified as being too costly and time-consuming with disputing parties having little to no control over the process or the extensive delays in court. Arbitration is the most widely accepted

[113] Kovač, p., 2016. izzivi alternativnega reševanja sporov v upravnih razmerjih v sloveniji in širše (challenges of alternative dispute resolution in administrative relations in a Slovenian and wider context). zbornik znanstvenih razprav, 76, pp.69-98.

form of ADR (Ellenberg, 2009). Recent discussion has argued that arbitration should not be considered as an alternative because arbitration has become too much like litigation (Jones, 1995). This is due to the judicial processes and control by strict legislation which usually involves representation by legal counsel.

The evolution of ADR techniques and their impact on construction developments has been significant in recent years. Evidence of this can be seen in the creation and revision of dispute resolution clauses in standard forms of contract. Many professional bodies and major building companies are involved in drafting standard forms of contract to provide a recognisable, equitable and flexible contract that can be applied to a wide range of projects. What confronts the industry is a multitude of ADR systems and hybrid techniques.

One of the challenges now facing the industry is to give more attention to dispute resolution clauses at the time of contract preparation and negotiation as best exemplified by Waldron (2006). There are a variety of ADR techniques in today's dispute resolution market: negotiation, mediation, early neutral evaluation, mini-trial (executive tribunal) and expert determination are considered below as being the most common.

7.4.1. Negotiation

According to Goldberg (2005) negotiation is by far the construction industry's favoured means of dispute resolution. It is a voluntary non-binding process of working out an agreement by direct communication. The process may be bilateral or multi-lateral, a particular advantage for construction disputes which often involve more than two parties. Where a negotiation is assisted by a neutral third party aiding the disputants toward settlement, this enters the realm of mediation. Many standard form construction contracts and other construction contracts for long-term or large-scale projects include dispute resolution clauses, which specifically provide for negotiation to escalate through various levels of management. These dispute escalation clauses often begin with a meeting between site representatives, progressing to meetings between directors, finance officers or other senior executives, all with a view to resolving the dispute[114]. This is a useful way of raising awareness of the dispute at more senior management levels. It creates the opportunity for a more objective assessment of the position by senior decision makers, thereby increasing the opportunity of settlement. A successful negotiation increases the chances of maintaining the relationship between the parties. However, negotiation can be used as a stalling tactic. The absence of a neutral party to manage the process may reduce the chances of reaching agreement, particularly in complex disputes or those involving many parties. In a sophisticated industry sector such as construction and infrastructure where the participants are well placed to identify and manage risks, there is every reason to expect parties to be able to reach a settlement through simple negotiation.

7.4.2. Mediation

Mediation is a process whereby the parties attempt to reach an amicable settlement with the assistance of an independent and impartial third party[115]. The mediator has no authority to impose a solution on the parties[116]. Mediation can be arranged at anytime, anywhere and at short notice. A mediator is appointed by the parties. There is no need for the mediator to be legally qualified. There are a number of initiatives

---

[114] Wilmot-Smith on Construction Contracts, 4th Edition 2021, [2.74]. Also see the discussion on the advantages and disadvantages of such clauses at Chapter 12 under 'Multi-tier dispute resolution clauses'

[115] The term 'conciliation' is frequently used interchangeably with mediation.

[116] See, for example, the International Mediation Institute, www.imimediation.org/about/, and the Civil Mediation Council, https://civilmediation.org/for-the-public/about-mediation/.

attempting to develop global, professional standards for mediators and advocates in mediation[117]. Mediation has also adapted quickly to the covid-19 landscape, recognising the efficacy of meeting online[118]. There is no set procedure for a mediation. It can take place online, by telephone or face-to-face. Many mediations have taken place online or with a hybrid form in the past year due to the covid-19 pandemic. The hybrid mediation can take many forms, such as where one party has some participants online and some together in one venue or all of one party's participants are together in a venue and others are online. The framework usually is established by the relevant provisions in the underlying contract, and in the mediator's appointment.

All mediation is broadly private and confidential, and where English law applies, is subject to the 'without prejudice' doctrine[119]. Mediation can be used in cases involving two parties and those involving multiple parties. There are two, possibly three, main types of mediation: facilitative, evaluative and transformative. In all cases, the parties are given the opportunity to voice their point of view. In a facilitative mediation, the mediator simply facilitates agreement between the parties. The mediator helps the parties to focus on the real issues in the dispute and find their own solution. He or she gives no view on the merits of each party's position nor of the likely outcome if the matter is ultimately decided by a judge or other final determiner. In an evaluative mediation, the mediator provides the parties with an assessment of the merits or the likely outcomes. These views are not

---

[117] United Nations Convention on International Settlement Agreements Resulting from Mediation.

[118] See, for example, the Joint COVID-19 Protocol established between the Japan International Mediation Centre and the Singapore International Mediation Centre, which provides for low fixed fees and online mediation, https://simc.com.sg/jimc-simc-joint-covid-19-protocol/,

[119] See *Halsey v. Milton Keynes General NHS Trust* [2004] EWCA Civ 576. This case has been cited in more than 60 authorities, which demonstrates the clear judicial determination to encourage ADR. There is a useful summary of the related subsequent case law in the White Book 2021, Vol. II, Section 14, Part 3 'ADR and Costs'.

binding unless the parties agree that they will be. In a transformative mediation, the mediator seeks to transform the relationship of the parties away from an adversarial and attritional relationship to a collaborative relationship. The mediator usually declines to offer a view on the merits of the dispute, but rather facilitates the parties to evaluate the strength of their position in relation to the other.

Generally, unlike the other two forms of mediation, transformative mediation happens almost exclusively in joint sessions. The parties agree which of these types of mediation should apply. They can change that approach during the mediation. Facilitative mediations are far more common than evaluative. Of the three, transformative mediation is the newest type or style. Mediation in many jurisdictions is not mandatory. At present, judges in England and Wales have no statutory or other power to order parties in a construction dispute to mediate. However, its use in England and Wales is generally strongly encouraged. An unreasonable refusal to mediate will be taken into account when determining costs, even in situations where a party is otherwise entitled to recover their own costs.

There is also judicial support in England and Wales for making an order for compulsory mediation – but no such order has yet been made in a construction dispute[120]. In contrast to this, various jurisdictions have adopted forms of compulsory mediation/ADR for civil disputes[121]. The international reach of mediation is demonstrated by the number of global providers of mediation services or rules, such as the International Chamber of Commerce (ICC) and the American Arbitration Association/International Centre for Dispute Resolution, together with more regionally based institutions, such as the Hong

---

[120] Sir Geoffrey Vos raised the possibility of whether the court might also require parties to engage in mediation despite the decision in Halsey, in McParland v. Whitehead [2020] EWHC 298 (Ch) [42].

[121] These include Italy, Ontario, Australia and Greece; see Civil Justice Council, Compulsory ADR, June 2021 [55] and its cited sources.

Kong International Arbitration Centre and Singapore Mediation Centre. The European Union actively promotes mediation. The principal objective of the EU Mediation Directive is to encourage recourse to mediation in the Member States[122]. Where EU law applies, it applies to cross-border disputes in civil and commercial matters. The main advantage of mediation is that it can produce a quick and cost-effective settlement. Insofar as there is data available, it seems to have a good success rate[123].

Referring a matter to mediation reduces the instances where a dispute leads to the termination of a commercial relationship. Mediation allows the parties to find their own solution, and to accept a range of outcomes broader than any court or arbitrator has the power to grant. The main disadvantage of mediation is that the resulting settlement agreement is only binding contractually. It is not directly enforceable in the courts. Its enforceability relies on the parties to honour the deal they have made. Where this does not happen, the parties remain in dispute and litigation may be necessary to enforce the settlement agreement or resolve the dispute entirely. This perceived weakness is now addressed by the United Nations Convention on International Settlement Agreements Resulting from Mediation, named the Singapore Mediation Convention. It entered into force on 12 September 2020, and at the time of writing, already has 54 signatories.

---

[122] Directive 2008/52/EC.

[123] The Centre for Effective Dispute Resolution (CEDR) Ninth Mediation Audit (launched May 2021) reports an aggregate settlement rate in civil and commercial disputes of 93 per cent, compared with 89 per cent in 2018. The proportion of cases that achieved settlement on the day of mediation was 72 per cent, not significantly different from the 2018 Audit, but there had been a marked increase in the proportion settling shortly after mediation, rising to 21 per cent of all cases compared to 15 per cent in 2018. It also reported on the impact of covid-19 on mediation – while there was a downturn in mediation activity with overall activity dropping by 35 per cent from March to September 2020, there was a very rapid surge in online mediation. There is no concrete data on whether online mediation has impacted the settlement rate of cases. CEDR quotes its own statistics as showing a 'circa 90% settlement rate for online mediations, something which is conferred, anecdotally by mediators', Thomson, 'The Ninth Mediation Audit – Five Things you Need to Know', www.cedr.com/the-ninth-mediation-audit-five-things-you-need-to-know/.

This includes the world's two largest economies, the United States and China, as well as several of the largest economies in Asia[124]. The Convention (and the related Model Law) aims to provide an efficient and harmonised framework for cross-border enforcement of mediated commercial settlement agreements[125]. Other problems with mediation are that, although less expensive than litigation, it can be expensive, particularly for smaller parties or projects. Further parties may take advantage of the mediation process to uncover the other side's case with no real intention to settle. Finally, there has been increasing focus on combined ADR procedures such as 'arb-med-arb'. Here, parties embark, even if only nominally, on an arbitration and request a sole arbitrator immediately to refer the dispute to mediation. The arbitration is stayed by a procedural order that refers it to a mediator. If the mediation succeeds, the resulting agreement is referred back to the tribunal, which issues an enforceable consent award. If the mediation is unsuccessful, the matter is returned to the tribunal, and in most cases the matter continues with limited time or cost having been incurred in ADR. This combined ADR procedure has been successfully adopted by the Singapore International Mediation Centre and the Singapore International Arbitration Centre. It can be written into a contract or agreed on an ad hoc basis once a dispute has arisen.

7.4.3. Early neutral evaluation

Early neutral evaluation (ENE) is a process whereby the parties instruct a neutral third party to provide a non-binding assessment of the merits of their claims. It offers the advantages of a private opinion on the merits of the dispute from an independent, respected and often expert source[126].

---

[124] See https://treaties.un.org/doc/Treaties/2019/05/20190501%2004-11%20PM/Ch-XXII-4.pdf,

[125] The final text of both are available on UNCITRAL's website.

[126] Bresco Electrical Services Ltd (In Liquidation) v. Michael J Lonsdale (Electrical) Ltd [2020] UKSC 25, per Lord Briggs JSC, [10].

There is no prescribed procedure for ENE, and the key elements of the process are likely to be set out in the underlying construction contract. ENE is usually conducted on a 'without prejudice' basis[127]. It may relate to factual disputes, technical issues, legal merits or a combination of these. The evaluator may be a judge, lawyer or expert. Many professional bodies maintain lists of approved evaluators[128]. The evaluation is privileged and non-binding, unless the parties agree otherwise. ENE may be used as a means to bring the parties directly to settlement, or may be followed by further forms of ADR. ENE can provide a quick, authoritative and objective assessment of the merits of a claim without incurring the costs of arbitration or litigation.

It can be particularly useful where the parties have very differing views of the prospect of success and an inadequate understanding of the risks of litigation itself. It can focus the parties' expectations of litigation, and offer a realistic indication of the likely outcomes. It narrows the issues to facilitate other forms of ADR. However, ENE may be less suited to disputes involving issues of fact where oral evidence needs to be heard. It is less likely to be useful in large complex disputes, where the necessary preparations may result in a process that is disproportionately expensive for a non-binding result. It may entrench the dispute and compromise further negotiation. Judicial ENE (where the evaluator is a judge) is very rarely used in the Technology and Construction Court (TCC) and commercial courts of England and Wales, although it is widely and successfully used in family law proceedings[129].

---

[127] See footnote 105

[128] For example, the Chartered Institute of Arbitrators, the Royal Institute of Chartered Surveyors or the Academy of Experts.

[129] Seals v. Williams [2015] EWHC 1829 (Ch) per Norris J.

7.4.4. Mini trial (or Executive Tribunal)

A mini-trial, sometimes known as an executive tribunal, is a non-binding, flexible form of ADR. Each party presents its case, usually by legal advisers, to a mini-trial panel. The panel normally consists of a company executive from each party, as well as a neutral third party who may act as a mediator or adviser. The executives who appear on behalf of the parties will not usually have been involved in the dispute, and should have sufficient authority to settle the dispute. The object of a mini-trial is to identify the strengths and weaknesses of each side's case as quickly as possible. The parties, or their legal advisers, make short and often informal presentations to the panel, all of whom are free to ask questions. Documents, including witness statements and expert evidence, can be exchanged in advance. Following submissions from each party, the panel will negotiate.

The role of the neutral on the panel is usually to provide advice on matters of law and evidence during the presentations, and to advise of the outcome in litigation if the parties fail to reach agreement in the course of the mini-trial[130]. The neutral may also act as a mediator between the two senior executives. The mini-trial process gives senior executives an opportunity to consider the legal arguments of both sides and to then negotiate settlement from an informed position, without relying on further legal procedures or remedies. It remains an uncommon form of alternative dispute resolution, even in the United States, where it originated in the 1990s. It is seen as being more suitable than mediation in very large cases or where it is

[130] See *Lomax v. Lomax* [2019] EWCA Civ 1467, in which the Court of Appeal ruled that the court has the power pursuant to Civil Procedure Rule (CPR) 3.1(2)(m) to order early neutral evaluation, even in circumstances in which one party had not consented to its use.

desirable to bring in senior executives who have not previously been involved with the case[131].

7.4.5. Expert determination

Expert determination is a process in which a dispute is submitted by the agreement of the parties to one (or more) independent experts who make a determination on the matter. Typically, the parties agree that the expert's decision will be final and binding except for a limited number of circumstances such as fraud, partiality or a material departure by the expert from his or her instructions[132]. The expert is permitted and entitled to use his or her own expert knowledge. Unlike a judge or an arbitrator, the expert does not decide matters solely on the basis of submissions and evidence put before him or her. Unless required by the parties, the expert does not have to provide reasons for his or her decision. An expert determination is a confidential process. It is particularly suited to disputes involving matters of valuation or those that involve technical issues. Expert determinations are entirely dependent and controlled by the agreement between the parties. There is no statutory basis or control of the process. Many institutions provide their own rules that may be incorporated into the contract, from the ICC to smaller transnational institutions such as the Resolution Institute in Australia and New Zealand. The main advantages of the process are that it is usually a quicker and cheaper process than litigation or arbitration, and the parties can create their own procedure. It allows parties to go straight to the expert without

---

[131] CPR, the International Institute for Conflict Prevention & Resolution, provides a Minitrial Procedure for use in a variety of circumstances, with a sample minitrial schedule, www.cpradr.org/resource-center/rules/international-other/mediation/cpr-minitrial-procedure.

[132] See, for example, *Flowgroup Plc (In Liquidation) v. Co-operative Energy Ltd* [2021] EWHC 344 (Comm), in which the court found that where parties had agreed to subject their dispute to an expert determination, a 'manifest error' exception within the contract allowed recourse to the court in only limited circumstances.

the involvement of a judge or arbitrator, who, in any event, may be reliant upon an expert for assistance in reaching a determination. The main pitfall of an expert determination is that if the expert reaches the wrong conclusions, the parties have very limited rights of appeal.

7.5. International experience of ADR

Fenn, O'Shea and Davies (2005) conducted an extensive survey of construction dispute resolution in 17 countries ending in 1998. It was found that mediation was hardly ever used or not recognised as a valid dispute resolution mechanism in seven countries: Italy, Ireland, Japan, Portugal, Romania, Scotland and Switzerland. Ireland used conciliation rather than mediation and Oman had no concept of non-binding dispute resolution. Mediation was increasingly used in Canada, Malaysia and The Netherlands. In Australia, Quebec and Sweden, mediation was widely used and effective. The value of mediation has also been widely acknowledged worldwide, as evidenced by the number of jurisdictions in which the courts enforce obligations on parties to negotiate and adopt mediation to settle construction disputes. A body of literature in the construction mediation field of course exists in many other jurisdictions, including England and Wales, Scotland, the USA, South Africa, Turkey and Australia.

The work undertaken by Brooker and Wilkinson (2010) demonstrated the continued & dramatic expansion of mediation in construction industries across many common and civil law countries. The majority of the case studies in the review indicate that their individual construction industries have been instrumental in the development of both government and industry policies for mediation. The review indicates that mediation developments are taking place extremely rapidly but not all countries are implementing mediation in the same way and the legal frameworks in some cases are substantially different. For example, some countries have approached ADR and mediation by introducing mandatory rules for its use. However, mandatory legal developments are not identical and even within different countries federal jurisdictions and courts adopt different approaches to the selection of cases for mediation (Aibinu et al, 2010). Both England and Hong Kong have developed similar Civil Procedure Rules to encourage mediation and use cost penalties to encourage parties to mediate (Brooker and Wilkinson, 2010; Cheung, 2010).

The review also reports on unique developments in some countries such as Turkey where the government is developing a legal framework to support mediation through a Mediation Act, which will regulate mediation practice and developments (Ilter and Dikbas 2010). Where significant mediation developments have taken place, the steer from industry and governments has taken different forms: For example:

- Many common law countries have implemented court rules to encourage or use mediation and penalties for non-use
- Some countries and specialised construction courts have their own mediation schemes or programmes to promote, govern and monitor activity
- Other countries or federal jurisdictions have developed mandatory mediation court programmes

The review also found that these initiatives inevitably led to developing legal jurisprudence concerning the validity of contract clauses or with providing statutory interpretation of the rules requiring or governing practice.

7.6. ADR in the UK construction industry

In 2006, the Centre for Effective Dispute Resolution (CEDR) dealt with a total of 691 cases, 8% of which were from the construction industry. While no recent disaggregated figures are available by industry in subsequent CEDR audits, Brooker and Wilkinson (2010) suggests 'that there are between 170 and 300 construction mediations [are] taking place annually'. Also precise numbers for mediations conducted in the commercial field are difficult to quantify in the UK. Whilst this number may appear small, this is not a negligible figure. In a study, Gould et al. (2009) suggests that construction mediation may actually be more prevalent than was previously supposed.

With there being a lack of any overarching reporting mechanism, the precise numbers of construction mediations in the UK can only be estimated. While the growth of ADR techniques in the international construction industry has not developed in the UK, there is also a marked divergence in ADR use, particularly between England and Scotland.

7.6.1. The English experience

The growth of mediation in the U.K. construction industry was slow. In one 1994 study only 30% of the surveyed respondents had ever been involved in an ADR process (Fenn and Gould, 1994). By 2002, however, one survey showed that 70% in construction had used ADR at least once (Brooker and Lavers, 2002). Genn et al (2007) claimed that *Dunnet v Railtruck* caused a distinct increase in take-up of the voluntary mediation scheme (VOL) in the Central London County Court. The increased use of ADR and mediation in practice was assisted by the Civil Procedure Rules[133] where the overriding objective was set out in Rule 1.1 as 'enabling the court to deal with cases justly'. Parties are obliged to achieve this objective by clearly setting out the issues in dispute, identifying key documents, and, in particular, attempting to avoid litigation by settling the dispute[134]. A claimant must comply with

[133] Civil Procedure Rules, London: Stationery Office, 1999, SI 1998/3132

[134] Practice Direction – Protocols 1.4 (2).

the Pre-action Protocol for Construction and Engineering Disputes before commencing proceedings in the court and, 'the court will look at the effect of non-compliance on the other party when deciding whether to impose sanction'[135].King's College London has sponsored a number of research papers in recent years relating to mediation practices in England. Gould's study into the use of mediation in the Technology and Construction Court 2006-2008 provided useful data. It showed that where mediation was successful significant cost savings were achieved by the parties. Only 15% reported savings of less than £25,000; 76% were in excess of £25,000; and the top 9% saved over £300,000. Cost savings were proportional to the cost of the mediation (Gould et al, 2010). The vast majority of mediations were undertaken on the parties own initiative and only 22% were court suggested or by Order of Court. Even where unsuccessful, nine out of ten mediations were as a result of the parties own initiative which supports the argument that court sanctions are effective and that advisors now routinely consider mediation as a viable option[136].

A significant finding was that parties decide to mediate at three key stages in the process: as a result of exchanging pleadings; during or as a result of disclosure; and shortly before trial. Of successful mediations, many parties thought that the dispute would have progressed to judgement had mediation not taken place[137].

The vast majority of mediators were legally qualified and only 16% were construction professionals. Only 20% of mediators were appointed by a Mediator Appointing Body and the rest were agreed by the parties[138]. There was also a tendency to use the same mediators again and again which indicated a mature market in mediation (Gould et al, 2010).

---

[135] Ibid.,Para. 1.4.

[136] Ibid., p. 50.

[137] Ibid., pp.47-48.

[138] Ibid., p. 51.

The nature of cases brought to mediation were: building defects, 18%; payment issues, 13%; professional negligence, 13%; and property damage, 13%. Mediations usually concerned only one matter and sometimes two (Gould et al, 2010). There was, however, a discernible change over time. Between 1999 and 2009 the number of cases relating to changes in scope of work, project delays and site conditions all decreased, whilst those relating to defective work and product and design issues increased significantly. Payment issues remained constant (Gould, 2009). It would appear that adjudication is good at settling disputes about variations, delays and site conditions[139].

There is currently no state control in England and Wales for the training, appointment and performance of mediators. There is, therefore, no moderation of courses or their contents (Gould, 2011). Accreditation is, in practice, required for practitioners who wish to gain a reputation in mediation to gain appointments. A European Code of Conduct for Mediators was developed for, but not incorporated into, the European Mediation Directive (Directive 2008/52/EC). The Code states that the mediator must be competent, neutral, available, non-conflicted, fair and give no legal advice. Mediators' advertising must be professional and accurate, and the mediator must carry professional indemnity insurance. Mediation must be voluntary and the parties and/or the mediator should have power to terminate the mediation at any stage (Boulle and Nesic, 2001). The Technical and Construction Court Settlement Scheme was introduced as a pilot scheme in June 2006 as a, 'confidential, voluntary and non-binding dispute resolution process'. The idea was to make use of the expertise of TCC judges as a result of their specialist knowledge (Gould, 2011).

139 Ibid., p. 8.

7.6.1.1 Change to the judicial approach to ADR

The English courts have power to use costs awards as a sanction against parties who refuse unreasonably to attempt ADR. This ability in the English Rules to encourage the use of ADR has been backed up by comment and orders from judges in a series of cases since 2000 culminating in the decision of the Court of Appeal in *Halsey v Milton Keynes NHS Trust* decided in May 2004[140]. The rationale for supporting judicial and legislative recommendations of using mediation and ADR processes is that if offers a more efficient and cost-effective system for the parties (and the courts are not clogged up with cases that could have been resolved otherwise)[141]. The reason for mediation and ADR processes being promoted in the commercial realm has been clearly espoused in *Aird v Prime Meridian Ltd*[142] where it was held that mediation is "a form of neutrally assisted negotiation"[143].

In this form of negotiation there is greater independence for the parties, because the process "need not necessarily be based on the underlying legal rights or obligations of the parties. Instead, the parties, with the assistance of the mediator, can reach a solution which is tailored to their real needs and interests"[144]. The inference is that mediation (and ADR processes) will be more capable of supporting the interests of the parties and coming to an amicable solution than objective and abstract judicial determination. Thus, this gives rise to the principle of co-optation within

---

[140] See also Court of Appeal in Burchell v Balland decided in April 2005, Wethered Estate Limited v Michael Davis and Others and Earl of Malmesbury v Strutt & Parker decided in March 2008 further examples where the English courts would not tolerate the unreasonable refusal to take part in mediation where the parties have contracted to mediate or where the courts consider it might achieve a settlement outcome.

[141] Lord Justice Jackson Review of Civil Litigation Costs Final Report (TSO, 2011) para 4.11

[142] Aird v Prime Meridian Ltd [2006] EWCA Civ. 1866

[143] ibid at 5 47 ibid at 5

[144] r. 1.1(1) CPR 1998

the CPR. The primary reason for co-optation is to enable the courts to deal with cases justly[145], which is best achieved through limiting the burden of cases that reach the judicial system. This is supported by r. 1.1(2) CPR 1998, which provides that alternative processes should be used when practical. The determination of practicality is based upon (a) equality; (b) saving expense; (c) proportionality in respect to the value of the claim, the importance of the case, complexity of the issues; and the financial position of each party; (d) assurance that the case is "dealt with expeditiously and fairly; and (e) allotting to it an appropriate share of the court's resources, while taking into account the need to allot resources to other cases". These factors will be examined by the courts, in order to promote mediation/ADR. However, it cannot force such processes on the parties. Rather, it may merely indicate that there may be negative cost implications for the failure to consider a more appropriate alternative to the judicial process.

Another area of uncertainty regarding mediation was that of enforcement, however yet again the courts in *Thakrar* (Peters, 2010) supported mediation by deciding that a settlement agreement obtained through mediation was valid and enforceable. Any hopes harboured that provisions for non-binding mediation setting no time limits were unlikely to be enforced by the English courts were squashed in *Cable & Wireless* (Clark, 2010).

Over the years alternative dispute resolution (ADR) systems have progressed, the introduction and implementation of the Civil Procedure Rules, changes in judicial approach and pre-action protocols often require parties to consider ADR before using adjudicative procedures. The recent introduction the Construction Industry Council Model Mediation Agreement and Procedure may

---

[145] r. 1.1(2) CPR 199

be a catalyst for ADR growth in construction and property sectors in England. However, the Scottish landscape is very different.

7.6.2. The Scottish experience

Agapiou and Clark (2011) surveyed Scottish construction lawyers' experiences and attitudes to mediation and found that 90% of respondents were able to explain mediation as an ADR process, 82% had received some form of training in mediation and, indeed, 18% were accredited mediators.

Two-thirds of the legal firms had a policy of encouraging mediation and only 18% had no policy at all. Almost all of those surveyed had experienced three or more mediations, 44% five or more and 21% ten or more. The types of disputes which were mediated were: payment issues, 29%; damages, 22%; professional negligence, 21%; changes to the scope of works, 11%; and delays, 10%. Settlement rates were high at 74% with a further 9% partially settled. Satisfaction were not so high with 63% often satisfied with the outcome, 43% with speed, 43% with cost and 50% with the mediator (Agapiou and Clark, 2011). The reasons for failure of a mediation were: entrenched or polarized positions; bad feelings between the parties; mediation attempted too late; and the lack of a skilled mediator.

Lawyers would, however, recommend mediation for its speed, cost, creativity, confidentiality, and purely tactical reasons. The reasons for refusing to mediate were: clients' wishes; lack of good faith; and a belief in the strength of the case (Agapiou and Clark, 2011).

The key skills of a mediator were considered to be: communication skills; the ability to build rapport and engender trust; empathy, flexibility and an open-minded approach; an understanding of the commercial and business environment; and legal skills and experience (Agapiou and Clark, 2013). Barriers to the development of mediation were: its relatively early development phase; the variable quality of mediators; the lack of stringent regulation; and the paucity of suitably experienced construction mediators. Barriers within the legal profession itself were: mediation does not comport well with comfortable, well-worn practice norms; lawyers are uncomfortable with the role of mediation advocate; and a cultural change shift is required before mediation will gain full acceptance (Agapiou and Clark, 2013).

Lawyers recognised that support for mediation by the Scottish judiciary was largely absent and gave little support for mandatory mediation. Lawyers noted, however, that mediation flourishes under pressurized or mandatory environments (Agapiou and Clark, 2013).

Lawyers found it difficult to predict settlement in mediation with factors such as prior relationships, value in dispute, and desired outcomes cited. As one lawyer said, 'it was not simple to say that certain dispute types or particular kinds of disputants rendered mediation more apt than others'.

Timing was held to be important (not too far down the line), but there was also a view that parties do not settle until brow-beaten by the travails of the legal system (Agapiou and Clark, 2013).

The ready access to now familiar statutory adjudication appeared to hamper the development of mediation. Adjudication was positively appraised as the natural port of call in construction disputes as it was quick and its decisions tended to be de facto final (Agapiou and Clark, 2013).

Although lawyers often control access to mediation and become buyers of mediation services, they believed that sophisticated clients and repeat players with in-house legal teams determined the dispute resolution process. Lawyers had more positive views of mediation than their clients and blamed clients for refusing to mediate. Parties were the real barrier to mediation according to lawyers (Agapiou and Clark, 2013).

In summary, lawyers recognised the need for institutional scaffolding, have little knowledge or experience or training in mediation, have concerns about fee income and see adjudication as a significant barrier to mediation.

Agapiou et al (2012) also surveyed Scottish contracting firms with a follow-up analysis of Scottish construction 'clients' who were, in fact, contractors and sub-contractors, not building sponsors.

These surveys showed that most respondents were aware of mediation but had little experience of it. Only one in five firms had a policy on mediation and, indeed, a few had a policy never to use mediation. Astonishingly, almost 90% of respondents had no exposure to mediator training and two-thirds had no experience of it. The types of dispute that were mediated included: changes to the scope of work; payment issues; and delays, professional negligence and damages. Settlement rates were high at almost two out of three with some partially settled. Satisfaction rates were high too with 80% satisfied with the mediator, 85% with costs, 93% with the process and 73% with the outcome.

Respondents particularly noted the cost savings compared with other dispute resolution processes, the collaborative atmosphere and that, perhaps for the first time, the decision-makers opposite became fully aware of the circumstances of the dispute. The majority agreed that settlements were complied with (Agapiou et al, 2012).

The reasons to mediate were: savings in cost and time; continued business relationships; creative agreements; the low value in dispute;

and the risks associated with continuing the dispute. The reasons for refusing to mediate were: cost; strength of their case; belief that negotiation could settle the dispute; and a fear of lack of good faith in opponents. The reasons for failure of a mediation were: an unwillingness to compromise; tactical use of mediation; the dispute was too personal; lawyer resistance to settle; and ignorance of and hostility to mediation. Surprisingly, it was reported that 46% of mediators offered their own opinions on the merits of the case (Agapiou et al, 2012).

Although almost half of respondents believed that the prominence of adjudication blocked out mediation, many complained about adjudication in terms of the poor quality of adjudicators, high costs and a threshold value in dispute of at least £50,000 to make it worthwhile (Agapiou et al, 2012). It is noted that, despite the hoped-for renaissance in arbitration following enactment of the Arbitration (Scotland) Act 2010, only 22 arbitrations were held in Scotland in the year to 30 June 2014, and many of them were agricultural (Aberdeen University, 2015). In summary, the take-up of mediation by contractors was low, awareness of its benefits was low and education, conferences, seminars and training are needed. Contractors are perhaps wrestling back control of dispute resolution processes from lawyers. The need for a legal framework to mediation is recognised, as are stiffer measures to drag parties to mediation (Agapiou et al, 2013). There was also a call for a Scottish Technology & Construction Court, but that is unlikely for want of business (Aberdeen University, 2015).

Trushell *et al* (2016) also investigated the attitudes and experiences of Scots Construction Mediator relative to the process, based on the small sample of practitioners in Scotland. Hitherto, much of the research in the Scottish context has focused almost exclusively on Construction Lawyers' interaction with Mediation, while no single study has adequately captured the attitudes and experiences of mediators themselves, their predilection for the process, their views on its benefits, and the optimal regulatory and statutory environment required for mediation's further promulgation as the most effective means of Dispute Resolution within the Construction Arena. Trushell et al's found that Mediators believe that process is a successful dispute resolution process because it is quick, cheap, flexible, creative, confidential, non-confrontational and applicable to almost all disputes.

The findings also revealed that a successful outcome depends on the skills of a good mediator, thorough preparation by all participants, the presence of key decision-makers, the parties' willingness to compromise, and the mediator's judicious application of pressure to settle. The Mediators surveyed also believe that clients' negative perceptions of mediation are a bigger barrier than lawyers' perceptions.

Interestingly, the findings of Gregory-Steven's research (2016) lend credence to this thesis, albeit based on evidence from South of the Border. Whilst accepting that a facilitative model was the purest form of mediation, about a third of the mediators were prepared to offer an evaluation of the dispute, possibly due to a substantial proportion being Quantity Surveyors with sound technical knowledge. All agreed, however, that the agreement of the parties was vital before an evaluation could take place. There was little support for mandating parties to mediate before proceeding to court action. The mediators wanted judicial encouragement for mediation backed by some legislative support, mediation clauses incorporated into construction contracts, and government adoption of mediation as the default process in its own contracts. Brooker and Wilkinson (2010) showed that mediation of construction disputes can flourish only with the active encouragement of government and its judiciary.

7.7. ADR compared with arbitration and litigation in construction disputes

Irrespective of the industry sector, settlement requires communication and a willingness to compromise. ADR can assist with both. The processes set out above give the parties in any commercial dispute an opportunity to communicate their understanding of the dispute to each other, and, if they wish, to seek an objective evaluation by an independent party of the strengths and weaknesses of their respective positions.

Except for adjudication and expert determination, these consensual processes of ADR can produce creative commercial solutions that are not available through litigation and arbitration. ADR is private, confidential, quick and flexible, as well as generally inexpensive. The flexibility of ADR was particularly apparent throughout the global covid-19 crisis. Parties accepted remote interactions with each other and neutral resolvers such as mediators in the face of national and international restrictions on meetings and movement. Even if ADR does not generate a settlement, it can help the parties refine and define the dispute, making it ultimately less costly to resolve. ADR permits the parties to collaborate to find a solution and to thereby preserve the commercial relationship.

One of the simplest ways to demonstrate an acknowledgment of the advantages of ADR is the fact that many courts around the world offer ADR as an adjunct to their own trial processes, whether as a prerequisite to litigation[146] or as an option for the parties[147]. Court-

[146] The EU Mediation Directive (2008) issued a demand for Member States to build mediation into their legal systems, which some Member States adopted as a requirement. For example, Italian law requires parties to attend what is called a 'required initial mediation session' for certain limited categories of disputes.

[147] Court-appointed mediators are available for certain disputes, usually in family law or for claims of less than £10,000 in England and Wales. In the United States, the Alternative Dispute Resolution Act of 1998 required all federal courts to establish some form of ADR, and granted the courts authority to send civil cases to ENE and mediation.

annexed mediation is particularly prevalent, and the courts in a number of countries offer judicial early neutral evaluation[148].

The Gregory-Stevens and Frame's (2016) study revealed that that the low-up take of mediation within the construction arena is due to the strong support for adjudication, lack of trust that the other party will act faithfully and the dispute will be compromised, and misconceptions that mediation is inappropriate or is not capable of solving the dispute. The authors highlighted the need for lawyers – as "Gate Keepers" – to engage with the move away from adjudication as the primary dispute method and encourage the use of mediation as the first step in the resolution of disputes.

Alternative Dispute Resolution does not suit all disputes. Certain complex disputes will need a full trial process with disclosure, witness statements and expert reports. There are others in which an important point of legal principle needs to be resolved in order to address the underlying dispute. Construction and infrastructure disputes in particular can be factually and technically complex. They can generate difficult points of law involving specialised forms of contract. They also frequently involve multiple parties, making it more difficult to reach agreement to use ADR effectively.

These disputes may still need to be finally decided by judges and arbitrators. Both litigation and arbitration have responded to the challenge of resolving construction and infrastructure disputes. Both have introduced procedural innovations to provide shorter and earlier hearings at reasonable and proportionate cost. Recognising the need for judges and arbitrators with industry experience, specialist

---

[148] In England and Wales, the court's power to order ENE is included with the Civil Procedure Rules (CPR 3.1(2)(m)), and in some states of the United States, such as California.

commercial courts are opening across the world such as in Singapore, Amsterdam, Paris, Frankfurt, Brussels, Dubai and throughout China However, ADR should be more attractive to the construction and infrastructure industry as a means of risk management. Disputes in this sector can be especially costly to litigate and arbitrate due to typically large volumes of documents and the use of expert evidence, in many cases across multiple disciplines and involving many participants. Typically, those involved with a construction project at the outset do consider the appropriate dispute avoidance and resolution mechanisms for the particular project, and these processes are incorporated within the contract between the parties. Many of the widely used standard forms in this sector, including FIDIC and NEC, provide for ADR.

The 2020 ICC Dispute Resolution Statistics show that a record number of new requests were filed with its International Centre for ADR under the ICC Mediation Rules. The disputes concerned a wide range of business sectors. Construction and engineering disputes accounted for almost 24 per cent of cases, followed by disputes relating to energy and telecommunications[149]. In the aftermath of the covid-19 pandemic, the 'massive economic advantages' that speedy and effective resolution of disputes provides should be particularly attractive to this industry sector. It can be the difference between solvency and insolvency. We may be about to reach the time when the construction and infrastructure sector stops talking about alternative dispute resolution, and dispute resolution edges towards becoming an integrated whole[150].

---

149 The value of disputes in all business sectors in 2020 ranged from a few thousand dollars to over US$800 million (with an average amount in dispute of US$66 million).

150 See the comments of Sir Geoffrey Vos, 'The Relationship between Formal and Informal Justice' (March 2021), [37]–[39], www.judiciary.uk/wp-content/uploads/2021/03/MoR-Hull-Uni-260321.pdf,

7.8. Court-annexed alternative dispute resolution

This procedure is one either initiated by the courts or directed by the procedural rules in a litigation process. Primary experimentation and development of the procedure occurred in the United States.

Various state and federal court jurisdictions began running pilot schemes in court annexed arbitration and other forms of ADR in the 1970's and 1980's with the objectives of reaching settlement without court intervention or as a minimum reducing the scale of the dispute.

The various schemes effectively cover the whole range of binding to consensual outcomes with the essential element that settlement is either achieved at this stage or where the initial finding is not binding the dispute continues along the continuum directly into litigation as the courts are already involved in the process. The U.S. Civil Justice Reform Act 1990 included ADR as one of a number of case management strategies designed to reduce cost and delay in civil litigation. This was followed by the Alternative Disputes Resolution Act of 1998 that required litigants to consider ADR giving the courts the power to compel the use of dispute resolution via Mediation or Early Neutral Evaluation[151]. In parallel with the move to formalise the structured processing of disputes another complementary technique was being tested, the Multi-Door Courthouse dispute strategy.

First evolved by EA Sander, a Harvard Law Professor in the 1970's, the Multi-Door Courthouse is a method of matching the dispute to the most effective mode of dispute resolution. Specially trained court officers under the guidance of the courts carry out the match-up

[151] Evaluation of Mediation and Early Neutral Evaluation under the Civil Reform Act, the Institute for Civil Justice, 1996

procedure with the objective being to satisfy the needs of the parties by designing the most effective procedure for their particular dispute. The over-riding benefit being savings in costs and time in reaching settlement. In a survey conducted by the District of Columbia to identify the key success criteria for the Multi-Door Courthouse system[152]. The five most important elements were; firstly to have a viable funding plan in place. Secondly to set up an administrative team who collectively had a clear understanding of the court process and the ADR portfolio. Thirdly to have an appropriate mix of volunteer and professional service providers. Fourthly to have the support of the judiciary and the legal profession. Finally to select the ADR procedure with care.

Court Annexed ADR and the Multi-Door Courthouse system have continued to evolve in the United States and there has been conflicting research results as to their efficacy. In major studies carried out by the RAND Corporation reported in 1996 and another by the Federal Judicial Centre in 1997 there was no clear evidence of measurable benefits in their use. RAND said of previous empirical research it studied on Court Annexed ADR;

> *"... the available findings could not provide an adequate basis upon which to make definitive policy recommendations .... mediation and neutral evaluation programs ... are not a panacea for perceived problems of cost and delay, but neither do they appear to be detrimental ... This lack of a demonstrated major effect on litigation costs and delay is generally consistent with the outcomes of empirical research on court related ADR"*

---

[152] Report to the Judicial Conference Committee on Court Administration and Case Management. A study of the five demonstration programmes established under the Civil Justice Reform Act of 1990, January 24, 1997.

These surprisingly neutral findings seemed to suggest that the jury remained out on the true benefits of this form of procedure. The Federal Judicial Centre took a more holistic approach to their findings, being guarded about judgement strictly on the statistical data and instead using other measures gleaned from various participant bodies that led them to conclude that in overall terms ADR did benefit dispute disposal.

Certain members of the jury on this form of ADR have, in fact, raised significantly dissenting voices on the approach. GT Eisele in his article "The Case Against Court-annexed ADR Programs"[153] was condemnatory of the procedure. He saw it as, in effect, an attack on natural justice in that it removed the right of a party to a dispute to have the matter tried in court. He felt voluntary participation in ADR was at the free choice of the parties but coercion was a step too far. He also argued strongly that the claimed savings for the ADR process were not founded in fact. In a telling observation he noted that without any use of ADR, records showed that over 90% of cases settled anyway before a trial took place with the 7-10% left requiring a trial to achieve justice.

Despite the limited recorded evidence to support the use of Court Annexed ADR, the overwhelming views of the legal profession and the judiciary were that this tool in case management was a benefit and the ADR Act of 1998 was seen as a clear endorsement of these views.

Other jurisdictions have followed the lead provided by the United States.

Canada has embraced the approach after successful test projects in various provinces. The Canadian Task Force reported significant

[153] (1991) 75 (1) Judicature 34, pp 35-37.

reductions in time to settlement for cases employing Mediation as a part of their case management strategy. The use of a Mediation procedure was mandatory unless one of the parties to the dispute could convince the presiding judge otherwise. Australia, among other Commonwealth States, has also embraced Court Annexed ADR. It has introduced mandatory mediation clauses into many of its legal and procedural statutes following a pilot scheme operated between 1987 and 1995 that yielded results that showed that a high percentage of cases referred, at first instance, to mediation settled at that stage.

The inherent dilemma of court-connection necessarily influences the nature of mediation when it is conducted within the litigation context. Nonetheless, court-connected mediation is not restrained from delivering some degree of responsiveness, self-determination and cooperation, which are core features of the mediation process and transcend the differences between theoretical notions of mediation. These core features are delivered to disputants through opportunities to explore a range of their own interests, participate directly and cooperate. There is some empirical evidence that has demonstrated that these key opportunities are denied to many disputants within some common law jurisdictions, most notably in Australia, nonetheless, this aspect of jurisprudence remains largely unexplored within the construction arena

7.9. Summary

This chapter reflects on how Adjudication, Arbitration and Litigation have altered the dispute disposal landscape in the Construction Industry and what lessons there are for the development of consensual or crossover forms of ADR into other areas of commercial dispute. In particular the model provided by Adjudication will be used to create proposals for alternative forms of structured non-judicial dispute resolution that have been designed to mix the best effects of Adjudication's evaluative procedure with the non-adversarial consensual ADR methods such as mediation.

This chapter also reviewed the external international influences with respect to the use of ADR and how the influence of multi-national commerce require that the English and Scottish systems must be capable of adapting themselves to the various forms of ADR favoured by organisations involved with inward investment or business with English and Scottish companies, public bodies or private individuals.

References

Aberdeen University (2015) The Scottish Arbitration Survey, Report No 1 (Edinburgh), p. 25.

Andrew Agapiou and Bryan Clark (2011). Scottish construction lawyers and mediation: an investigation into attitudes and experiences. International Journal of Law in the Built Environment, 3(2), pp.159-181.

Andrew Agapiou and Bryan Clark (2012), 'An empirical analysis of Scottish construction lawyers' interaction with mediation: a qualitative approach', Civil Justice Quarterly, vol. 31, no. 4, p. 499

Andrew Agapiou, Bryan Clark and Gerry Keegan (2012), 'Construction Disputes and Mediation: a study of the attitudes and experiences of Scottish contracting firms', Royal Institution of Chartered Surveyors COBRA Conference, 10-13 September, Las Vegas, Nevada, USA, pp. 24-25.

Andrew Agapiou and Bryan Clark (2013), 'A follow-up empirical analysis of Scottish Construction Clients' interaction with Mediation', Civil Justice Quarterly, vol. 32, no. 3, p. 379.

Aibinu, A.A., Akin-Ojelabi, L. and Gardiner, B., (2010). Construction mediation in Australia. In Mediation in the Construction Industry (pp. 33-59). Routledge.

APS Group Scotland (2019) An International Evidence Review of Mediation in Civil Justice, PPDAS598390 (06/19). Available at: https://www.gov.scot/publications/international-evidence-review-med

Astor, H and Chinkin, C (1998) in Fenn, P Davies, E, O'Shea, M (Eds) (1998) Dispute Resolution and Conflict Management in Construction: An International Review, p147.

Barlow J, Cohen M, Jashapara A and Simpson Y (1997) Toward positive partnering, Policy Press.

Barrick, M., 1998. Huge partnering savings identified. Building, 6, p.13 (1998).

Bennett J and Jayes S (1995), Trusting the team: the best practice guide to partnering in construction, Centre for Strategic Studies in Construction, Reading University.

Bowes, D., 2008. Identifying barriers to the establishment of dispute boards in UK construction. In Proceedings of 24th Annual ARCOM Conference, Cardiff (2008).

Bresnen, M & Marshall, N (2000) Partnering in construction: a critical review of issues, problems and dilemmas, Construction Management and Economics, 18:2, 229-237, DOI: 10.1080/014461900370852

Bresnen, M. and Marshall, N., (2002). The engineering or evolution of co-operation? A tale of two partnering projects. International journal of project management, 20(7), pp.497-505.

Brooker, P. and Wilkinson, S. eds., (2010). Mediation in the construction industry: an international review.

Lawrence Boulle and Minyana Nesic (2001), Mediation: Principles, Process and Practice (London: Butterworths, Routledge. p. 437.

Campbell, P (1997) Construction Disputes: Avoidance and Resolution, Whittles Publishing, Caithness, p65.

Cheeks, j.r., (2003). multistep dispute resolution in design and construction industry. journal of professional issues in engineering education and practice, 129(2), pp.84-91.

Cheung, S.O., (2010). Construction mediation landscape in the civil justice system in Hong Kong. Journal of Legal Affairs and Dispute Resolution in Engineering and Construction, 2(3), pp.169-174.

Clark, B. (2012) Lawyers and Mediation. Springer-Verlag, Berlin

Davies, E., Fenn, P. and O'Shea, M., (2005). Dispute Resolution and Conflict Management in Construction: An International Perspective. Routledge.

Ellenberg, C., (2009). Lie detection: a changing of the guard in the quest for truth in court. Law & Psychol. Rev., 33, p.139.

Eubanks F and Bruno G (1995) Partnering: The Construction Management Method of the Future, American Professional Constructor, September.

Gardiner, J. (2014), Latham's Report: Did it change us? http://www.building.co.uk/lathams-report-did-it-change-us?/5069333.article

Evans, M., 2018. Rethinking Legal Aid: an independent strategic review.

Genn, H., Fenn, P., Mason, M., Lane, A., Bechai, N., Gray, L. and Vencappa, D., (2007). Twisting arms: court referred and court linked mediation under judicial pressure. Ministry of Justice Research Series, 1(07).

Genton, P.M., (2002). The role of the DRB in long term contracts. Construction Law Journal, 18(1), pp.8-19.

Goldberg, S.B., (2005). The secrets of successful mediators. Negotiation Journal, 21(3), pp.365-376.

Gould, N., (2009). The mediation of construction disputes: Recent research. Disp. Resol. Int'l, 3, p.185.

Gould, N (2011) Alternative Dispute Resolution Workshop (London: Institution of Civil Engineers), p. 21

Hamza, A., (2002). Partnering in the construction industry: an empirical investigation into the critical success factors (Doctoral dissertation, Nottingham Trent University (United Kingdom))

Hawkins, D.E., (2013), Contracts versus Collaboration: Conflict or complementary (Exploring the relationship between contracts and collaboration

Hughes, D. Williams, T. and Ren, Z. (2012), Differing perspectives on collaboration in construction, Construction Innovation, Vol 12 Iss 3 pp355-368

Ilter, D. and Dikbas, A., (2010). Construction mediation in Turkey. In Mediation in the Construction Industry (pp. 147-167). Routledge.

Jones III, I.R., (1995). The Federal Arbitration Act and Section 2's Involving Commerce Requirement: The Final Step toward Complete Federal Pre-emption over State Law and Policy-Allied-Bruce Terminix v. Dobson. J. Disp. Resol., p.327.

Lamont, Z., (2001), February. Performing through partnering. In proceedings of the institution of civil engineers-civil engineering (vol. 144, no. 1, pp. 3-3). Thomas Telford house, 1 heron quay, London e14 4jd, England: Thomas Telford services ltd.

Latham, M. (1994), Constructing the Team, London: HMSO

Peters, D. (2010) It Takes Two To Tango, and Two To Mediate: Legal, Cultural and Other Factors Influencing United States and Latin American Lawyers; Resistance to Mediating Commercial Disputes Rich. J. Global L. and Bus. Vol 9, pp. 381-429

Robertson, E, Edinburgh (2018). Fit for the Future: Report of the Independent Review of Legal Services Regulation. Available at: https://www2.gov.scot/About/Review/Regulation-Legal-Services

Ross, M.L., (2021). Designing mediation for Scottish Civil Courts: Options and opportunity. Journal of Strategic Contracting and Negotiation, 5(1-2), pp.60-75.

Scottish Consumer Council (2001) Consensus without Court: Encouraging Mediation in Non-Family Civil Disputes in Scotland. Glasgow: Scottish Consumer Council

Scottish Executive (2005) Modern Laws for a Modern Scotland. A Report on Civil Justice in Scotland, Scottish Executive, ISBN: 978-0-7559-5110-9

Scottish Mediation (2019) Report of the Expert Group on Mediation in Civil Justice in Scotland, s.l.: Scottish Mediation. Available at https://www.scottishmediation.org.uk/wp-content/uploads/2019/06/Bringing-Mediation-into-the-Mainstream-in-Civl-Justice-in-Scotland.pdf

The Royal Society of Edinburgh (2002) Encouraging Resolution – mediating patient/health services disputes in Scotland, The Royal Society of Edinburgh, ISBN 0 902198 386, p.19

Waldron, B.D., (2006). Company Law & Governance Update

Wamuziri, S. and Seywright, A., (2005), Risk Sharing and effective incentives in collaborative procurement. In: Khosrowshaki, F (ed.), 21st Annual ARCOM Conference, 7-9 September 2005, SOAS, University of London. Association of Researchers in Construction Management, Vol. 2, 1175-1184

Wood, G. and McDermott, P., (1999). Searching for trust in the UK construction industry: an interim view. Profitable partnering in construction procurement, pp.107-116.

Xiaolong Xue, Qiping Shen and Zhaomin Ren (2010), Critical Review of Collaborative Working in Construction Projects: Business Environment and Human Behaviours, Journal of Management in Engineering 2010.26:196-208

Chapter Eight: The Facilitative Approach to Construction Mediation Practice

8.1 Introduction

Mediation is a method of conflict resolution which utilises an objective third party to assist the parties to resolve their conflict and thereby reach agreement (Foster, 2003). It therefore operates as an alternative means of dispute resolution from the traditional court process, which the parties voluntarily enter into. Whilst mediation has historical reference dating back to the Romans and probably was in existence even before this, as a means of alternative dispute resolution (ADR), it is relatively new (Barrett and Barrett, 2004). It was introduced in the 1990s to reduce the burden on the court system and was intended to provide a more cost effective and faster dispute resolution process for the parties .(Bevan et al, 2013). The move towards mediation was as a direct result of Lord Woolf's recommendations to reform the legal system were implemented by the Civil Procedure Act 1997 and the Civil Procedure Rules 1999. The key objective of the reforms was:

> *"to encourage the early settlement of disputes through a combination of pre-action protocols, active case management by the courts, and cost penalties for parties who unreasonably refused to attempt negotiation or consider ADR (Advice Service Alliance, 2014).*

It is the early settlement of disputes that mediation sought to achieve through the facilitation of a discussion between the parties and thus resolving the dispute prior to any adversarial action. The process of achieving resolution is therefore largely achieved with the mediator determining areas of common ground and in doing so enable the parties to focus on reaching a mutual resolution of the issues.

"The goal of mediation is to isolate contentious issues so that the parties can contemplate possible solutions and arrive at a consensual settlement (Daiker, 2005)."

This chapter seeks to argue that mediation is not achieving the intended objective in respect of reducing costs. In order to achieve this it will look at the various types of mediation that are available and assess them in respect of their implications on the court process. It will ask whether mediation should be mandatory and if so whether any particular type of mediation should prevail.

8.2. The theoretical model of mediation

The key principles of mediation are its voluntary nature, flexibility, impartiality and confidentiality. A wide range of models of mediation exist although in the main mediation uses a similar process as principled negotiation of identifying issues, considering the options and recording agreement.

Although there is no set procedure for mainstream mediation, it generally takes the form of the parties meeting the mediator in plenary session. The mediator will describe the process of mediation which may be unfamiliar to the parties, his role in the process, the need for confidentiality, his inability to act as a witness in any future trial, and the possibility of separate meetings with each party. Each party is then invited to state its view of the dispute and its hopes and aspirations for the mediation. The mediation process may then start immediately, but in commercial mediations the parties are likely to go to separate rooms which the mediator will visit in turn and work with them to tease out the issues in conflict before trying to generate options for consideration by the parties towards a resolution of the conflict. It may be beneficial for each party to meet the mediator in caucus to resolve individual issues privately. When agreement is reached the terms of settlement are drafted and signed by the parties to confirm their agreement.

Not all disputes, however, lend themselves to settlement by mediation. Where the dispute rests on a point of law a party may require a decision by a court in preference to compromising a firmly held belief that they are correct in law. Personal injury cases seldom go to mediation as most settle by negotiation between the two parties. Matrimonial disputes in which physical abuse has taken place are also seldom mediated due to the fear of the abused meeting the abuser. Mediation requires disputants willing to comprise their positions to reach settlement and if one party is unwilling to compromise then mediation is unlikely to be successful. Hibbert and Newman possible trial positions; equitable settlements depend on full discovery which results in delay and costs; its non-binding nature; use of delaying tactics; quick resolutions are prone to error and unfairness; uncertainty as to privilege of disclosures; and inequality of bargaining position and representation.

One criticism of mediation is that it is too focused on making a deal by urging parties to compromise. In striving to reach a settlement the rights and wrongs of a dispute may be overlooked just to do a deal. There may be no legal basis or foundation classic critique holds that informal justice, such as mediation, increases capacity of those already advantaged. Although a central tenet of mediation is that the mediator is neutral and impartial, Hippensteele asserts that one cannot assume the neutrality of a mediator.

A further criticism of mediation is that it lacks transparency. The strictures of confidentiality inhibit the accumulation of knowledge about the practice of mediation.

Interestingly, the findings of Chakley and Green (2016) research, lend credence to this thesis. The findings of this theoretical, meta-analysis indicate that mediator neutrality has no consistent or comprehensible meaning and is not capable of coherent application in the construction sphere. It also seems, in the view of Chakley and Green (2016), that the requirements for mediator neutrality can encourage covert influencing tactics by mediators which itself threatens party autonomy.

The authors also conclude that mediator intervention ensures: (i) ethical and moral implementation of justice; (ii) removal of epistemological implications of subjective fairness; and (iii) compensation for lack of pure procedural justice in the mediation process. In addition, that party autonomy requires mediators to intervene ensuring: parties adequately informed of the law; and equal balance of power

8.3. Types of mediation

On the basis that mediation can apply to any dispute between parties and thus serves a wide-ranging application, it has been necessary to adopt different styles or categories which treat the meditative process very differently. In this regard, there are four primary categories of mediation which offer distinctly different approaches to the mediation process and potential outcome for the parties (Foster, 2003). It is hoped that by assessing the distinctions between the mediation styles that a discussion into the benefits and issues of a given style will emerge and enable conclusions to be drawn in respect of which, if any, is more suitable.

8.3.1. Facilitative mediation

The facilitative meditative process was the first mediation style adopted and was developed to ensure that the parties reached a mutually acceptable resolution to the conflict. It still operates as the primary type of mediation currently in use and thus it is generally considered to be largely successful (Zumeta, 2014). In essence a facilitative mediator is focused on enabling the parties to "communicate with and understand one another" (Waldman, 1998). In this respect, they avoid any reference to coercive behaviour and do not therefore advise the parties on the form of action to take. Braithwaite describes facilitative mediation or facilitation as enabling "both sides to see the middle way" (Braithwaite, 2013). Thus the "facilitative mediator assumes that his principal mission is to clarify and to enhance communication between the parties in order to help them decide what to do" and therefore any outcome that is achieved is purely reflective of the parties' discussions (Brown, 2004).

The mediator achieves this by asking questions that will enable both parties to understand the merits of their arguments in addition to the relative strengths of their cases (Riskin, 1996).

Naturally, the fact that the mediator does not offer or "give advice, recommendations or opinions" means that they remain completely impartial to the dispute resolution process.(Foster, 2013)

The findings of Trushell et al's (2016) investigation into the attitudes and experiences of construction mediation practitioners chime well with Foster (2010) comparative study of mediation styles. Indeed, of the 11 mediators interviewed seven said they were facilitative, three were evaluative and one used both techniques. The evaluation style was closely related to mediators' primary profession as a quantity surveyor.

One respondent said:

> *'.what [the parties] wanted, which is familiar in the oil industry, is effectively a deal broker, a banger, bum kicker whatever you want to call it and that's what they wanted and that is what the oil industry general preferred and I suspect the sort of mainstream construction*

industry would probably, I guess, prefer that to a touchy-feely mediator'.

Another respondent said:

'....I can't say I am too precious about that, I think that really comes down to what the parties require from you. I think a facilitative process is by far the gold standard which you would want to aim for, but very often in the commercial construction disputes I am involved in some form of evaluative input by the mediator is helpful to the parties in moving them to a conclusion'.

One of the key criticisms of the facilitative approach are that the parties are not directed towards settlement of their dispute and therefore should the mediation process fail, the parties' costs from the mediation and subsequent court process will have escalated (Linden, 2004). In addition, there is criticism in respect of front loading whereby costs of reports and professional fees are added to the case at a fairly early stage (front loaded) which can effectively negate the benefits of the mediation process in respect of reducing costs (Law Society, 2010).

McDermott and Obardd (2004) highlight that whilst the facilitative method of mediation offers a:

"higher satisfaction rating for both parties in almost all procedural due process and distributive measures, [it] results in much less money obtained in settlement".

Naturally, many conclusions can be drawn from this in respect of the claimant lacking sufficient skill and knowledge by themselves to bring a favourable conclusion to their case. Nonetheless, it demonstrates the greatest potential to reduce parties' costs and this is greatest when counsel have not been instructed. Ultimately, though, one has to question whether the claimant would be as satisfied with this process if they were aware that, under the evaluative model, they were likely to achieve a greater award (McDermott and Obardd, 2004).

8.3.2. Evaluative mediation

The evaluative mediation style operates in stark contrast to the facilitative style in that the mediator actively participates in enabling the parties to reach agreement. In this respects Zumeta (2014) highlights that the "evaluative mediator assists the parties in reaching resolution by pointing out the weaknesses of their cases, and predicting what a judge or jury would be likely to do". Whilst it is true that mediators often will have some form of legal qualification or at least some form of experience within that field, this approach is often criticised on the basis that the mediator is effectively performing a more adversarial role in which they are insufficiently qualified (Foster, 2004). Others such as Riskin (1996) loosely contend that evaluative mediators are "qualified to give such guidance by virtue of ... [their] training, experience, and objectivity", Stulberg (1997), however, rightly points out that the facilitative mediator could be as, if not more, knowledgeable than the evaluative mediator but through the structure of the facilitative mediation does not impart this information to the parties. In this respect, it could be considered impossible for the facilitative mediator to enable the parties to truly understand the strengths of their respective cases if they did not have some experience or knowledge of the issues that they face. What is difficult to argue, is the adversarial nature of the evaluative model of mediation in respect of the typically higher awards received by the claimants (McDermott and Obardd, 2004). The findings of Wall et al's (2016) study confirmed that experiences acquired by individuals when working in different disciplines within the construction industry strongly influences the way they think and behave as mediators when mediating disputes.

In terms of style, it seems that lawyer mediators favoured an evaluative style to increase the prospects of achieving a settlement in an attempt to reduce the risk of the dispute escalating into litigation, whereas non-lawyer mediators favoured a facilitative style and were of the opinion that the evaluative model should be avoided due to the risk of impinging on the parties' ability to self-determine their own dispute, which is the principle underpinning a successful settlement in mediation. There were also differences of opinion noted between the lawyer-mediators and non-lawyer-mediators in terms of ability and skill to manage conflict and to more effectively mediate construction disputes.

8.3.3. Transformative mediation

The transformative style of mediation closely resembles the facilitative style in terms of the structure of the process but it nonetheless seeks to ensure that the parties understand the others respective viewpoints and thus seeks to empower the parties in their decision making (Foster, 2003). Linden (2014) provides a more definitive distinction between the facilitative and the transformation styles by stating that the communication elements are not restricted to the words and tone that the disputants use. This therefore places emphasis on the "body language and attitudes of the disputants" which he contends" is central to the Transformative style"(Linden, 2014) In respect of the similarities between the facilitative and transformative styles of mediation it is noted that they attract criticisms of a similar nature:

> *"Detractors say that facilitative and transformative mediation takes too long, and too often ends without agreement. They worry that outcomes can be contrary to standards of fairness and that mediators in these approaches cannot protect the weaker party". (Zumeta, 2014)*

8.3.4. Narrative mediation

Narrative mediation is derived from narrative therapy developed by Billikopf-Encina (2002); it seeks to break the conflict cycle by devising it in terms of a narrative that can then be altered to the needs of the parties. The mediator in this instance is seeking to encourage the parties to look objectively at the issues one step removed from the conflict that has arisen (Foster, 2003). Linden (2014) highlights that this method "tries to use conversation and discussion to get the disputants to disclose, often unwittingly, the true nature and perception of the conflict". However; he also highlights that this form of mediation is particularly well suited to instances where the parties will continue the relationship after the conflict is resolved.

8.3.5. Mediating construction disputes: Facilitative vs Evaluative models of practice

A review of construction mediators' codes of practice suggests that the majority have adopted the EU Mediator Code but this does not constrain mediator styles and an inspection of mediation contracts commonly used in England and Wales indicates that the process is in the hands of the mediators who should be guided by the parties or their lawyers but the rules are often prescriptive and legalistic in design (Brooker, 2011).

Research suggests that there are few construction mediators in England and Wales who practise purely transformative mediation and a review of training and mediator profiles indicate that it is likely that most use a mix of facilitative and evaluative techniques (Brooker, 2007; Brooker, 2011). As mediation is more closely connected to litigation, research in England and other parts of the UK indicate that evaluation is often an integral part of mediator practice and construction mediation has not been immune to this development

(Brooker, 2007; (Agapiou and Clark, 2011)). Evaluative mediation has the effect of reducing self-determination as mediators take control of the process by providing settlement options, evaluating the 'strengths and weaknesses' of the participants' cases or 'predict' likely outcomes at court (Kovach and Love 1996, 1998; Welch 2001 (a)(b)). Brooker raises concerns that parties in England Wales engage in mediation without sufficient 'informed consent' about such issues as confidentiality and self-determination which generates further doubt on party autonomy (Brooker 2011; 2013).

Whilst accepting that a facilitative model was the purest form of mediation, about a third of Construction Mediators surveyed by Trushell et al (2014), were prepared to offer an evaluation of the dispute, possibly due to a substantial proportion being Quantity Surveyors with sound technical knowledge. All agreed, however, that the agreement of the parties was vital before an evaluation could take place. This finding is important given the fact that Agapiou (2013) found a significant number of respondents signalling a desire for more evaluative mediation strategies. This holds significant implications for mediation training in Scotland most of which follows a general facilitative mediation model.

8.4. Issues with mediative approaches

Much research has suggested that construction mediators desire judicial encouragement for mediation backed by some legislative support, mediation clauses incorporated into construction contracts, and government adoption of mediation as the default process in its own contracts (Trushell et al, 2014; Wall et al, 2016).

These findings chime with that of Brooker and Wilkinson (2010) who showed that across a multitude of jurisdictions mediation of construction disputes can flourish only with the active encouragement of government and its judiciary.

Whilst mediation is not currently mandatory, there are implications imposed if the parties choose not to undertake mediation. Clause 1.2 of Practice Direction - Pre Action Conduct specifically requires the parties "exchange information about the issue, and consider using a form of Alternative Dispute Resolution ('ADR')". Failure to comply with the provisions enables the court to take this into consideration when determining matters of costs[154]. Furthermore, there are clear directions that the parties need to undertake these assessments regardless of whether the Practice Direction applies directly[155]. Nonetheless, it is cases such as *Coventry and others v Lawrence and another* that suggest pre-action meditative provisions are not fulfilling their intended objective in respect of reducing parties' costs and hence call into question the application of mediation as a means of ADR[156]. The implications of this are that the costs that the parties may face from the resulting litigation could far outweigh any potential award that can be made and could also potentially exceed the parties' means to pay them (Bickford-Smith, 2014).

Mediation, however, has much to offer the parties in that it offers a cost-effective resolution to conflict in around 80 percent of cases and, in this respect, has a high success rate (Bevan et al, 2013). Nonetheless, when we frame the term success, we are merely assessing it on the resolution of the issue or conflict and not in accordance with the how satisfied the parties or disputants were with the process (Waldman, 2013). Furthermore, satisfaction itself can be framed in a number of ways i.e., mutually desirable outcome or greater award and in this regard could itself create conflict (McDermott and Obardd, 2004) What is most notable is that the studies of mediation are fairly restrictive

---

[154] Practice Direction - Pre-Action Conduct, Cl. 4.1.

[155] Ibid, Cl. 6.

[156] *Coventry and others v Lawrence and another* [2014] UKSC 13.

and thus cannot give an outright determination of which category of mediation performs best for the parties and thus should become the preferred option.

In Trushell *et al's* (2014) investigation of the attitudes and experiences of construction mediators', respondents were equally divided in their answer to the question, 'is mediation about just settlement, or just about settlement'. Five mediators thought mediation was about just settlement, five thought it was just about settlement and one challenged its relevance as it was up to a party to refuse to agree to something which was unjust. Those mediators who thought it was just about settlement supported the view that mediation was all about getting a deal. No party could be forced to agree to something with which it disagreed, Parties only agree to a settlement with which they can live with. Justice, therefore, need not come into the settlement.

The contrary view of some mediators was that if both parties reach a win-win situation and settle, then that is a just settlement. Some mediators thought there was more to a good mediation than merely reaching settlement, such as the repairing or the re-creation of business relationships. Indeed, one of the respondents philosophized as follows:

> *'I think the difficulty with the word settlement is it is a connotation for a legal result which is rights based, claims based and often money based. Meditation is about so much more'.*

Many of the issues stem from the confidentiality of the process which prohibits analysis of mediator performance, the approach of mediation, the meditative rules or whether it should indeed be compulsory for the parties to attempt mediation prior to court.

The confidentiality of the mediation process has many disadvantages as is now being recognised in other forms of ADR such as arbitration and hence decisions in certain arbitral hearings are now being reported with the parties' details removed as a means of ensuring transparency and consistency (Trushell et al, 2014). In this regard Brown identifies:

> *"If fairness, particularly to an underrepresented group, is elusive where the outcome is leveraged by legal rights and decision-making is open to scrutiny, the prospect of fairness without those features seems doubly dim"(Brown, 2010).*

In respect of arbitration, the time and cost reduction benefits initially sought by the parties are less likely to be achieved and may even be higher, than that if the parties had chosen to go to court to resolve their dispute (Bhatta et al, 2009).

Whilst it is conceded that there are other benefits to arbitration in respect of choice of law and jurisdiction to be applied; if the mediation process was to follow the same path of increasing costs, it is difficult to envisage that its benefits would be maintained over that of the court process. The evaluative style is similar to that of the arbitral hearing but most importantly does not incorporate a ruling and hence it could be argued that the same level of transparency is not required.

Nonetheless, with costs increasing as is particularly evident in the evaluative style, surely it is important for the parties to be able to assess the benefits of one mediator over another in terms of their successes. The lack of reporting standards or regulatory body would indicate that whilst information may be presented, it may not be done in a way that can be compared or contrasted with other mediators and thus is unlikely to enable the parties to make an informed decision..

Brown (2004) supports the facilitative approach to mediation in respect of the creation of "new dimensions" that can lead to the resolution of the parties' issues in a manner that allows the parties to uncover "shared compatible interests". Nonetheless, its validity over the court process remains an issue for example; Braithwaite applies (2013) the facilitator in a personal injury context, and highlights that issues can be created in respect of potentially limiting the parties access to funds. This is due to the mediator focus will steer the claimant towards publicly funded resources as opposed to the insurer seeking to meet some of the costs. Furthermore, he contends that issues in respect of the quantity of interim damages that can be claimed, often requires "lawyers [to] front-load the work, because they have to present a compelling case for an interim payment". Unfortunately, this has the effect of ensuring that the costs spiral, but there is little to contend that this would be different should the evaluative style have been used instead of the facilitative approach.

The decision in *Eeles v Cobham Hire Services Ltd* highlights the complexities involved in respect of interim payments for equipment and accommodation that cannot be fully determined until a much later stage[157]. In this regard, it is possible to argue that the meditative process may not be well suited to certain disputes.

Incorporating the legal representation costs, to the costs of the mediator and evidence demonstrates that the costs will begin to escalate. This has led all forms of mediation to be subject to the criticism of front loading.

The effects of this could reduce the benefits of the mediation process to such an extent that it becomes a much less viable option for the parties over the court process:

> *"Such evidence as there is indicates that the Woolf reforms are working, to the extent that pre-action protocols are promoting settlement before application is made to the court; .... However, costs have increased, or have at least been front-loaded. In particular,*

[157] Eeles v Cobham Hire Services Ltd [2010] 1 W.L.R. 409.

in cases where mediation has been attempted and agreement has not been reached, costs are clearly higher for the parties " (Advice Service Alliance UK, 2014).

The natural conclusion to draw in this respect is that the facilitative approach does not steer the parties towards agreement and therefore could result in the parties being subjected to these higher costs. However, there is also evidence to suggest that the evaluative form of mediation encourages higher costs in its reliance of legal advisors and evidence that essentially creates the issue of frontloading. Nonetheless, the evaluative process which seeks to steer the parties to resolution and is thus structured in a far more adversarial manner raises concern that mediation is becoming the 'poor man's' court through the creation of a tiered resolution approach in which access to the courts require greater financial reserves.

What is evident is that there are few empirical studies into the effectiveness of mediation or the benefits of one style of mediation over another: no study to date has examined disputant satisfaction when participating in an evaluative mediation as opposed to a facilitative mediation (Waldman, 1998). Moreover, where research has been conducted the findings suggest that the results are inconclusive, in that some suggest that the outcome of the mediation will not vary substantially with a particular style of mediation, whilst others suggest that mediation styles can significantly alter the outcome (McDermott and Obardd, 2004). Without further research in this area one method cannot be truly proffered against another as more beneficial and in this respect many discussions focus on the potential benefits of utilising more than one style within a meditative process.

The lack of research is beginning to be addressed and hence studies by Brooker and Wilkinson (2010); Agapiou and Clark (2012); Agapiou (2013); Trushell et al, (2014) and Wall et al (2016) have been undertaken to improve access to mediation within the construction arena. This research however, is based on the perceived need to increase access to mediation in preference over that of arbitration and litigation.

This review argues that without an in-depth analysis of the construction mediation that has been undertaken to date and comparison into cases of a similar nature that went to court; the statements in respect of the mediation benefits do not hold up to scrutiny.

This is also true in respect of the differing mediation styles, one may be more beneficial than another or it may be more useful to utilise more than one style in a particular set of circumstances.

8.5. Summary

The assessment into the facultative model of mediation against the other models that are widely used prompted a debate into ongoing benefits of ADR measures over that of the courts. It has highlighted that whilst mediation was aimed at reducing costs and time that would be expended under a court process; the issues in respect of front loading and legal advice suggest that the previously envisioned cost benefits are diminishing to such an extent that the true benefits of mediation are being called into question. In this respect, the facilitative method offers the parties the maximum opportunity of reducing costs in that there is no requirement to be legally represented as the aim of the process is to seek agreement between the parties. The mediator does not steer the process but merely facilitates the communications between the parties. On the basis that mediation can apply to any dispute between parties and thus serves a wide-ranging application, it has been necessary to adopt different styles or categories which treat the meditative process very differently. In this regard, there are four primary categories of mediation which offer distinctly different approaches to the mediation process and potential outcome for the parties: facilitative, evaluative, transformative and narrative. While it may be argued that all disputants are transformed to some extent in all mediations, it is the Facilitative Model that is by far the modus operandi within the construction context.

References

Advice Service Alliance UK (2014), Civil Justice Since the Woolf reforms – how useful is ADR? [Online] Available at: <http://asauk.org.uk/policy/policy-2005/civil-justice-since-the-woolf-reforms-how-useful-is-adr/>

Agapiou, A and Clark, B (2011) Scottish construction lawyers and mediation: an investigation into attitudes and experiences, International Journal of Law in the Built Environment, 3(2) ISSN: 1756-1450

Agapiou, A (2011) Scottish Construction Lawyers' awareness and experiences of ADR, Proceedings of the Institution of Civil Engineers – Procurement, Management and Law, 164 (4), 181-192, ISSN: 1751-4304.

Agapiou, A and Clark, B (2012) An empirical analysis of Construction Lawyers' interaction with Mediation: a qualitative approach, Civil Justice Quarterly, October, ISSN: 0261-9261

Agapiou, A and Clark, B (2013) A follow-up empirical analysis of Scottish Construction Clients interaction with Mediation, Civil Justice Quarterly, July, ISSN: 0261-9261.

Agapiou, A (2013) The impact of legislative change on adjudication provisions and the requirements for written contracts under the Construction Act, US-China Law Review, 6 (13), ISSN:1548-6605

Agapiou, A and Clark, B (2014) A reflection on Construction Mediation in Scotland, Proceedings of the Institution of Civil Engineers – Procurement, Management and Law, 167 (6), p 265-272, ISSN: 1751-4304.

Agapiou, A (2015) The factors influencing mediation referral practices and barriers to its adoption: A survey of construction lawyers in England and Wales, International Journal of Law in the Built Environment, vol. 7, issue 3, p. 231-247. ISSN: 1756-1450

Bhatia V, Candlin C and Sharma R (2009), 'Confidentiality and Integrity in International Commercial Arbitration Practice 75(1) Arbitration 2.

Barrett J T and Barrett J P (2004), A History of Resolution: The Story of a Political, Cultural, and Social Alternative Dispute Movement (John Wiley & Sons xxvi.

Bevan A, Hollebon G and Bromfield L (2013), Mediation: A Practical Guide (Thorogood Publishing) 11.

Bickford-Smith J (2014), 'The Costs of Complexity: A Practical View from the Bar' Littonton Chambers [Online] Available at: <http://www.littletonchambers.com/the-costs-of-complexity-a-practical-view-from-the-bar-618/>

Billikopf-Encina G (2002), 'Narrative Mediation: A New Approach to Conflict Resolution' 13(1) International Journal of Conflict Management 100.

Braithwaite B (2013), 'Court-Free Catastrophic Claims Management and Resolution or Catastrophic Injury Claims without Recourse to the Courts 3 Journal of Personal Injury Law 190, 193.

Brooker, P., (2009). Criteria for the Appropriate Use of Mediation in Construction Disputes: Judicial Statements in the English Technology and Construction Court. Int'l JL Built Env't, 1, p.82.

Brooker, P. and Lavers, A., (2005). Mediation Outcomes: Lawyers' Experience with Commercial and Construction Mediation in the United Kingdom. Pepp. Disp. Resol. LJ, 5, p.161.

Brooker, P. and Lavers, A., (2005)a. Construction lawyers' experience with mediation post-CPR. Construction Law Review, 1, pp.19-46.

Brown C (2004), 'Facilitative Mediation: The Classic Approach Retains its Appeal' 4(2) Pepperdine Dispute Resolution Law Journal 279, 280.

Burns S (2008), 'Thinking about Fairness & Achieving Balance in Mediation' Fordham Urban Law Journal 35, 39.

Chalkey, K. and Green, M. (2016), "In the context of mediation, is safeguarding mediator neutrality and party autonomy more important than ensuring a fair settlement?", International Journal of Law in the Built Environment, Vol. 8 No. 2, pp. 161-175. https://doi.org/10.1108/IJLBE-10-2015-0016

Daiker M (2005), No J.D. Required: The Critical Role and Contributions of Non-Lawyer Mediators 24(3) The Review of Litigation 499, 450.

Davidson F (2011), 'The Arbitration (Scotland) Act 2010: The Way Forward or a Few Missteps?' 1 Journal of Business Law 43, 62.

Foster K (2003), 'A Study in Mediation Styles: A Comparative Analysis of Evaluative and Transformative Styles' [Online] Available at: <http://www.mediate.comarticles /fosterK1.cfm>

Linden J (2004), 'Mediation Styles: The Purists vs. The "Toolkit"' [Online] Available at: <http://www.mediate.com/articles/linden4.cfm>

McDermott P and Obardd R (2004), 'What's going on in Mediation: An Empirical Analysis of the Influence of a Mediators Style on Party Satisfaction and Monetary Benefit' 9 Harvard Negotiation Law Review 75, 76

Riskin L (1996), 'Understanding Mediators' Orientations, Strategies, and Techniques: A Grid for the Perplexed' 1 Harvard Negotiation Law Review 7, 28.

The Law Society (2010), 'A Summary of Sir Rupert Jackson's Final Report' 40.

Stulberg J (1997), 'Facilitative versus Evaluative Mediator Orientations: Piercing the 'Grid' Lock' 24 Florida State University Law Review 985, 997

Trushell, I, Clark, B and Agapiou, A (2016) Construction mediation in Scotland: an investigation into attitudes and experiences of mediation practitioners, International Journal of Law in the Built Environment, vol. 8, issue 2. ISSN: 1756-1450.

Waldman E (1998), 'The Evaluative-Facilitative Debate in Mediation: Applying the Lens of Therapeutic Jurisprudence' Marquette Law Review 155, 156.

Zumeta Z (2014), 'Styles of Mediation: Facilitative, Evaluative and Transformative Mediation' [Online] Available at: <http://learn2mediate.com/resources/styles-of-mediation/>

Chapter Nine: Conclusions

This evaluation has traced the history, development, current status and future direction of alternative dispute resolution in the UK construction industry. It is inspired by and draws on the largest collection of Royal Institution of Chartered Surveyors-funded research on English and Scots disputants' perceptions and attitudes to alternative dispute resolution.

The construction industry is famed for its litigious nature. In undertaking studies of these disputes, it is possible to categorise the nature of the dispute into a spectrum of common scenarios. There is much literature produced that reviews the nature of the construction industry highlighting how it is fragmented and that this leads to dispute. Whilst this is true, there is also the tendency of organisations to treat a win over a dispute as a measure of success or of how well someone is performing.

As the construction industry often calls for work that is of a specialist nature, main contractors often have to rely on the services of specialist subcontractors. In order to dispose themselves of risk, main contractors often use these subcontracts to pass the risk down the chain. This can result in complex subcontracts being put in place which are often not properly understood by those agreeing to them which increases the likelihood of dispute. Historically, relationships between organisations within the construction industry are often fuelled with mistrust and an unwillingness to share information. It is the secretive nature of these relationships that lead to the key players in the organisations becoming frustrated and suspicious of the other party. This perception of a hidden agenda can increase the likelihood of disputes arising. There is a general worldwide acceptance that the severity of disputation is higher in the construction industry than in other major sectors of the economy. There is also widespread recognition that because of the high incidence of disputes, the industry is an accepted leader in the development of dispute resolution systems and processes. The UK is seen to be at the forefront of dispute resolution techniques.

The objective of this text was to identify and evaluate the various forms of ADR in construction disputes, with a particular focus on mediation, arbitration, adjudication and litigation. Several conclusions may be drawn. The first relates to ADR more broadly, in that it has developed into a widely-used means of dispute resolution that is considered to have significant advantages over litigation. This is particularly the case for construction disputes.

The construction sector is one of the largest industries, particularly in the UK and so gives rise to the largest number of disputes. ADR has also been recognised in the international arena, with the result that various regulations, rules and standard form contracts have emerged which provide for the resolution of disputes through ADR.

The construction industry embraced the fast-track forms of dispute resolution and this quickly led to a transformation of the way disputes were dealt with (earlier, quicker and cheaper) but maintained a disputes culture. This ADR framework has become increasingly complex and detailed, to respond to new issues that arise and to further promote the resolution of disputes through ADR rather than litigation.

The text reviewed the role and function of the Technology and Construction Court (TCC) in the resolution of construction disputes. The case law of the TCC is demonstrative of its facilitative approach toward ADR in general and it adopts a rigorous approach toward parties who refuse to submit their dispute to ADR based on the principle of unreasonableness. The TCC has proven able to impose a coherent concept of reasonableness to distinguish between circumstances in which a party justifiably or unjustifiably refuses to resort to ADR given the circumstances of the case. Finally, the evaluation examined the example of time-related disputes, given that they are a particularly common form of construction dispute and emphasise the importance of time in construction projects. Construction projects are often linked to the phrase 'time is money' because they involve extremely high costs.

The main forms of ADR exist on a spectrum, depending on the extent to which a third party intervenes in the process. Negotiation lies at one end of the spectrum, in that it does not involve the intervention of a third party and enables the parties to the dispute to exert complete control over the process. The willingness of the parties to negotiate and the absence of a third party promote maximum cooperation. In the commercial world, negotiations are typically swift, enabling disputes to be resolved in a matter of days whilst maintaining the relationship between the parties. Thus it may be particularly effective for commercial and construction disputes which often involve underlying contracts that are long-term and time-sensitive.

Mediation involves a third party whose task is to assist the parties. The mediator does not arbitrate the dispute or determine the final outcome. Mediation is suitable for disputes that are context-specific, such as commercial and construction disputes. Such disputes do not involve issues relating to justice and rights, which are typically resolved through litigation. In the construction industry, mediation provides for the identification of commercial practices that are specific to the field. It is also typically much quicker and cheaper than litigation, meaning that a dispute may be swiftly resolved in time-sensitive projects, without damaging the parties' underlying commercial relationship.

Adjudication involves a neutral third party's decision, which is binding. Thus, adjudication exists between mediation and arbitration on the ADR spectrum. It is not uncommon for adjudication to be used as a method for resolving construction disputes and the use of an adjudicator is provided for in many standard form contracts used in the construction industry. This is helpful as the construction industry involves highly industry-specific practices. Appointing an expert adjudicator ensures that the dispute will be resolved appropriately and with underlying knowledge of the context of the dispute. It is for this reason that adjudication is a popular form of ADR for construction disputes.

Having examined the use of ADR in the construction industry both North and South of the Border, more benefits than disadvantages were identified. Since the late 1980s, it had been apparent that conventional litigation was too cumbersome, slow and expensive for certain types of disputes, particularly construction disputes. It was due to this that ADR developed for the resolution of disputes in this sector.

The key benefits of ADR for construction disputes are that it is swift, cost-effective, tailored to the dispute and the needs and expectations of the parties and promotes the preservation of their business relationship. Parties prefer ADR because they perceive it to be more creative and focused on the objective of problem-solving than litigation, which is based on the adversarial, rigid 'win-lose' outcome.

Overall, it is apparent that ADR has various advantages when compared to litigation in resolving construction disputes. A key advantage is that construction disputes generally require specific expertise and knowledge. ADR is more effective than litigation in recognising and responding to the time-sensitive nature of construction agreements. This also enables the parties to potentially continue with the underlying construction project without expensive delays. The speed of ADR has been directly linked to cost savings in the construction industry. Although there are some costs involved, these do not typically surpass the costs involved in litigation.

Finally, ADR offers the parties a private method of resolving their dispute which is particularly valuable because it does not pose a risk to their professional reputation.

It is due to the benefits of ADR for construction disputes that standard forms of contracts such as the JCT and FIDIC now provide for ADR. The revised FIDIC Red Book has proven particularly effective in not only promoting the use of ADR for construction disputes but also in preventing disputes from arising in the first place. It has created a distinction between dispute resolution and claims by placing them into two separate clauses, thus emphasising that a dispute does not automatically arise simply because a claim has been submitted.

Having examined the role and function of the DAAB, the evaluation concludes that it is an extremely important mechanism in the adjudication of construction disputes. It facilitates mutual agreement between the parties if an issue arises which could potentially lead to a dispute. Experience shows that it promotes cooperation and trust, positive relationships and open communication between the parties because it handles disputes individually, which reduces unresolved claims and avoids the development of a negative relationship or atmosphere. DAAB members have great construction expertise and experience which ensures that any decision made is more accurate. The existence of the DAAB also has a positive effect in terms of preventing claims from developing into disputes. Finally, it is independent and impartial, meaning that the parties will be more likely to accept its decisions. It provides a means of insurance for parties, enabling them to potentially resolve any dispute that could arise and to prevent disputes from arising in the first place.

Adjudication has developed into a particularly effective method for resolving construction disputes because the adjudication framework has developed considerably. Although adjudication is not intended to provide a final outcome, but rather a fast, temporary resolution, the majority of disputes sent to adjudication do not proceed to litigation or arbitration as the parties tend to accept the adjudicator's decision as final. This is indicative of the particular benefits and successes of adjudication in resolving construction disputes.

The effectiveness of adjudication is further promoted by the application of the rules and principles of natural justice. It does not evade the rules of natural justice that are applied to other forms of dispute resolution, namely arbitration and litigation, and its rules of adjudication are sufficiently detailed to ensure that the process is fair and the adjudicator's role is clear. This minimises the potential for parties to challenge the outcome of adjudication in the courts, which would undermine the benefits of adjudication.

With respect to dispute avoidance and resolution, a maxim which is frequently expressed is that 'prevention is better than cure'. In terms of dispute avoidance, there have been numerous industry initiatives in the UK since the late 1980s which have sought to identify the problems of the industry and then develop strategies and actions to achieve a cultural shift away from an adversarial culture. The industry has been repeatedly admonished and encouraged to embrace modern management concepts such as partnering and alliancing with an emphasis on early involvement in the decision-making process by key stakeholders including clients, contractors and building users. The relatively recent emergence and rapid uptake of alliancing, early contractor involvement, dispute/conflict avoidance schemes is testament to a movement toward the creation of dispute-averse relationships.

The fundamental premise is that the likelihood of disputes occurring will be significantly reduced if a proactive project environment can be created in which change management is an accepted tool.

In recent years, the construction industry has sought to develop a number of collaborative practices through contractual mechanisms designed to encourage the timely sharing of information and the ethos of working together as a project team. Many standard form construction contracts are designed to operate as a 'project management tool' used throughout the life of the project, as opposed to a document that is consulted only during challenging, adversarial times.

Construction contracts now have provisions that facilitate dispute avoidance and claims handling, to prevent disputes escalating through formal dispute resolution procedures and effective procedures aimed to encourage early amicable solutions, lower costs and fewer delays to the project overall. Multi-tiered dispute resolution clauses have come to be recognised as a commonly accepted method of dispute resolution clauses in commercial contracts - they often find place in construction contracts. The latest editions of the FIDIC, NEC4 and JCT forms each contain escalating dispute resolution procedures (in differing forms) and these procedures have now become mainstream. Typically, such escalating provisions involve an initial referral to senior executives or directors followed by either mediation (by agreement) or a form of adjudication or expert determination procedure and then either arbitration or court. The inclusion of these types of clauses are more a statement of intent than clauses that create binding contractual rights and obligations – certainly in common-law jurisdictions. However, the fact that they have now made their way into these contracts is further evidence of a shifting in approach.

There has also been an increase in the number of multi-party forms of contract in the market. The first in the UK was PPC2000. It has not been widely used but it was followed by the JCT Constructing Excellence Form in 2006 and, more recently, by the NEC4 Alliancing Contract. FIDIC is also considering developing a multi-party form. The uptake of these is most likely to be driven by the necessity of a more collaborative approach as we move forward with technological developments such as BIM, where the full benefits are only likely to be realised by all parties working together to design, build and thereafter operate and maintain buildings. In that environment the current two-party contracting is likely to be found not fit for purpose. Clearly, further changes in both dispute resolution and forms of contracting will be driven by the market and advances in technology.

Mediation is being used to rather great effect in the UK construction industry, when it is indeed used. The uptake of mediation, from the data provided, admittedly is low and has the potential to be possibly overly positive, simply due the fact that many parties who partake in mediation become repeat players. It is acknowledged that steps have been taken by the judiciary to attempt to improve mediation uptake (in the main to reduce court costs and increase efficiency), however to the Woolf reforms do go farther to promote the use of mediation than the Gill review in Scotland. The inclusion of mediation clauses within standard form contracts would no doubt increase the use of mediation within the construction industry just as was witnessed when adjudication was introduced. Standard forms of contracts are the "bread and butter" of the UK construction industry and though they are often amended heavily, the general principles of the contract are generally adhered to. Some may be surprised that the NEC3 contract does not already contain such provisions due to its emphasis on working in a spirit of mutual trust and cooperation. However, at the moment the only ones which even mention mediation are JCT and the SBCC (the NEC3, JCT and SBCC are the main suites of contracts used in the UK construction industry) and none state the mediation should be a mandatory first step in the dispute resolution process.

There is a clear indication from stakeholders that old-style dispute resolution is not the preferred route for the construction industry. The arbitration institutions, governments through statutory adjudication regimes and the standard form contract drafting bodies are providing a framework for a new approach to meet that demand. Although standard form contracts seek to avoid such disputes and despite the existence of principles of best practice in construction contract programmes, most construction projects suffer delays. Having examined the mechanism for resolving time-related disputes, it is clear that the FIDIC Red Book is a key method for preventing such disputes from arising because it offers detailed guidance on what is required to substantiate a claim, which is a clear advantage that the Red Book has over the Silver Book which lacks such detail, something which increases the potential for disputes, further delays and the need to resort to dispute resolution. This also demonstrates that effective guidance on such matters is key to minimising the potential for disputes. Detailed guidance also prevents employers from delaying evaluations of claims in bad faith, which further contributes to reducing the potential for disputes. The courts' evaluation of claims and assessment of delay damages appears to be appropriate, demonstrating their ability to identify and respond to the reality of such disputes.

The bulk of research seeking to explore the views and experiences of key actors relative to mediation is also often concerned with the legal profession rather than clients or other players in the dispute resolution game. Nevertheless, recent surveys of Lawyers & their Clients in England and Scotland has confirmed mediation a suitable forum for such disputes; the opinion being it can be effective in all types of construction disputes irrespective of the relationships involved. Based upon a meta-classification framework analysis of research in the field, Artan-Ilter's (2016) state-of the art review reveals that much of the construction mediation research in the past decade has focused on perceptions of professionals on mediation, the dynamics of the mediation process and mediator tactics.

The research highlights that while writings include important contributions regarding many aspects of construction mediation practice, the scholarship lacks a holistic agenda to overcome the key challenges to the widespread use of mediation in the construction sphere. The authors propose that academic community should re-focus and re-direct its efforts towards a research agenda that encompasses court-connected mediation, mediation in public projects, project mediation, documentation of case studies of mediation applications and use of IT in the mediation process.

References

Ilter, D.A., (2016). A research roadmap for court-connected mediation. Court-Connected Construction Mediation Practice: A Comparative International Review, p.111.

Index

www.ingramcontent.com/pod-product-compliance
Ingram Content Group UK Ltd.
Pitfield, Milton Keynes, MK11 3LW, UK
UKHW041133071026
15587UKWH00009B/470

9 781804 410868